MOLLY BROWN *from* HANNIBAL, MISSOURI

HER LIFE IN THE GILDED AGE

KEN *and* LISA MARKS

THE History PRESS

Published by The History Press
Charleston, SC 29403
www.historypress.net

Front cover: Courtesy of Steve Chou. The portrait of Molly Brown is from History Colorado.

Back cover, from top down: Courtesy of History Colorado; Courtesy of Steve Chou; Courtesy of the Library of Congress; New York Times photo from 1912; *Courtesy of the Hannibal Convention and Visitors' Bureau; Courtesy of the Library of Congress.*

First published 2013

Manufactured in the United States

ISBN 978.1.60949.871.9

Library of Congress CIP data applied for.

Notice: The information in this book is true and complete to the best of our knowledge. It is offered without guarantee on the part of the author or The History Press. The author and The History Press disclaim all liability in connection with the use of this book.

To Ella and Mary Kathryn,

whose indelible Irish spirit lives on
and whose Irish eyes still smile
in the memory of those who loved them best

Contents

Preface

She was born into a midwestern family with Irish roots and little money. She died an internationally known personality who had lived a life of fame and fortune that few would ever experience. In between, she fought for women's rights, juvenile justice and eight-hour workdays. She helped build a cathedral and saved a poet's cottage. She helped secure the right for women to vote and ran for the U.S. Senate. She was lauded by the French and attended the coronation of an English king. This was the incomparable Margaret Tobin Brown.

In April 2012, we were asked to make a presentation to children in the gifted program at Veterans Elementary School in Hannibal, Missouri, to commemorate the 100th anniversary of the sinking of *Titanic*. We knew a good deal about Molly Brown from visiting her birthplace in Hannibal, now open as a museum, and from the biography written in 1999 by Dr. Kristen Iversen, *Molly Brown: Unraveling the Myth*. But after sharing a brief summation of Margaret's life with the schoolchildren, we began to realize that hers was a story that needed to be told. So many of her accomplishments were unremembered, hidden by the long shadow cast by *Titanic*.

We began to sponsor events at the Hannibal History Museum to educate visitors about the amazing accomplishments of Margaret Tobin Brown. Remarkably, one of the first things people would say is, "What does Molly Brown have to do with Hannibal?" Most people didn't realize that she was born and raised in Hannibal—or that she was even from Missouri, for that matter. The common notion was that she was from Colorado.

Preface

It quickly occurred to us that the recollection that most people have of Molly Brown's story comes from the 1964 MGM musical starring Debbie Reynolds, *The Unsinkable Molly Brown*. Our younger guests only knew the story of Molly Brown from the 1997 movie *Titanic*, written and directed by James Cameron. We knew the movie well, but it had been years since we'd seen the musical, so we bought a copy of the DVD to see how they depicted her childhood in Hannibal. The movie musical begins with a shot of an infant, maybe nine months old, floating down the Colorado River in a wooden cradle. The fictional back story was that this child had survived a flood that had taken the lives of her mother and father, leaving her orphaned. A mountain man plucked the infant from the cradle to safety (proving that she's "unsinkable") and raised her as his own daughter in the frontier woods of the Rocky Mountains. Missouri was not even mentioned!

As we continued to share Margaret's *true* life story, we were always surprised at how enthusiastic our guests were about the tale and how many questions they had, eager to learn more. They would tell us that they had no idea how remarkable her accomplishments were and how surprised they were to hear how much more there was to her life story than just the sinking of *Titanic*. They were surprised that she had never been called "Molly" during her lifetime (the term "molly" is simply a euphemism for a young Irish lass and was not assigned to Margaret until after her death). And, of course, they were surprised that she was born and raised in Hannibal.

Margaret is certainly not the only famous person from Hannibal, Missouri. In the Hannibal History Museum, there is an exhibit of "Prominent Hannibalians" that celebrates other important personalities. There's a fellow named Mark Twain, who spent his boyhood in Hannibal and made the town famous in *The Adventures of Tom Sawyer* and *Adventures of Huckleberry Finn*; Cliff Edwards, star of stage and screen and best known as the voice of Jiminy Cricket singing "When You Wish Upon a Star" in the 1940 Disney film *Pinocchio*; Bill Lear, who cofounded a company named Motorola and invented the car radio, eight-track cassette and the Learjet; impressionist painter James Carroll Beckwith; Hall of Fame baseball player Jake Beckley; and many more.

During tours and lectures, we joke that there is something in the muddy water of the mighty Mississippi River that must contribute to these larger-than-life personalities, and certainly none was larger than Margaret Tobin Brown. But when you think of it, what was it about her childhood in Hannibal that prepared her for the amazing journey her life would take? What was the culture of Hannibal like during her years here that would shape her personal values and beliefs, the foundation built during her formative years that would spur her on to champion human rights and civil liberties throughout her life?

What follows is an attempt to not only tell the real story of Hannibal's own Margaret Tobin Brown but also examine the circumstances that occurred during her childhood that give us a greater understanding of what motivated her to rise from humble beginnings along the banks of the Mississippi to the highest echelons of society. When put into the historical context of her life and times, her escapades are even more remarkable; today, it is difficult to imagine the obstacles she would have had to overcome to pursue her ambitious goals, let alone to accomplish her extraordinary achievements.

This book will not serve as a complete, exhaustive biography of Margaret, but we hope that it will shed some new light and encourage the reader to learn more about this remarkable woman. Her humor, her down-to-earthiness, her common-sense approach and her courage and calm under duress would have been learned while living in the three-room house on Denkler's Alley. It was Hannibal that Margaret returned to year after year to reconnect with her roots, and she never forgot nor apologized for where she was from.

For you see, she may have *lived* in Denver, Colorado. She may have *lived* in Newport, Rhode Island, and Paris, France. But she was *from* Hannibal, Missouri!

Acknowledgements

This book would not have been possible without the generous contributions of so many who work tirelessly to preserve history. Bits and pieces of information regarding the remarkable history of Margaret Tobin Brown's life have been gathered, verified and preserved over the years by countless collectors, researchers and historians, and it is because of their generosity in sharing this information that we are able to tell the story that follows. We are inspired by their dedication.

We are so grateful for the love and support of our family: our sons, Jordan and Shea; our parents, Terry and Alice; and our uncle, Frank. Thank you for understanding what it means to us to be able to pursue our dreams and for giving us the support to help make them come true. To Buster and Lily Pearl, thank you for the warmth, humor and unconditional love you provide on a daily basis.

As always, our most sincere gratitude to our friend Steve Chou, the keeper of all things Hannibal. We are certain that we speak for thousands of Hannibalians when we say "thank you" for your dedication to preserving Hannibal's history and your generosity in sharing it with us. This book, as well as so many other projects that we've been fortunate to be a part of, would not have been possible without your assistance.

Special thanks to Nicole Rousch and the staff of the Molly Brown House Museum in Denver, as well as the entire staff of the Denver Public Library's Western History/Genealogy Department, for allowing us hours of joyous discovery when rifling through your files. We are sincerely grateful for your hospitality and generosity in sharing your collections with us.

To the staff of the Stephen H. Hart Library and Research Center at History Colorado, we thank you for your assistance in combing through box after box of the Lawrence P. Brown Collection. Special thanks to Jen Dibbern for helping us locate the "Suitcase with the Scrapbook," which proved to be an invaluable resource that gave remarkable insight into the ties that bound the Brown family together over the years. You went above and beyond, Jen, and we are so grateful!

Thank you to National Mining Hall of Fame and Museum director Bob Hartzell and to Judge Neil V. Reynolds for helping us understand Leadville's amazing history and for giving us a vision of the environment that Margaret would have found when she stepped off the train from Hannibal. We were delighted to spend time with you during our inspirational visit to Leadville.

To Jane Fehlmann-Garland, Ferne Fehlmann-Kurtz and Mary Rose "Momo" Shearer, owners of Avoca (aka the Molly Brown Summer House Museum in Denver), your family has had to sacrifice so much to preserve J.J. and Margaret's beloved ranch over the last eighty-five years, yet your love of the land and devotion to its preservation has never wavered. You are truly an inspiration, and your passion for Avoca is infectious. We look forward to many years of association with you and your family.

To the members of Friends of Historic Hannibal and the Marion County Historical Society, we appreciate your dedication and your unwavering support. Thank you all so much.

We are thankful for the support of the board and staff of the Missouri Humanities Council and appreciate the efforts of its executive director, Geoff Giglierano. Thank you for helping us bring Molly's story to life.

It all began when we received a request from Tracy Murphy, Veterans Elementary School Gifted Program facilitator, and Gail Bryant, director of the Hannibal Convention and Visitors Bureau, to present Molly's story to the children in Tracy's program. Thank you for giving us the nudge toward what has become one of the most rewarding chapters of our career.

To the staff of The History Press—including Ben Gibson, Jaime Muehl, Katie Parry and Ryan Finn—thank you for continuing to allow us the opportunity to share our stories. Third time's the charm!

Very special thanks to John and Candace Klemann. When you look in the dictionary under "tireless," you see their portraits. Your endless contributions to women's issues, children's needs, the celebration of the arts and historic preservation are so appreciated, and they are so much in keeping with the efforts put forth by Margaret Tobin Brown herself. You touch so many lives in so many ways; for us personally, you serve as mentors, friends, confidants and trusted allies. Thank you for all that you do.

To Jim and Sheryl Love, who are our most ardent benefactors, thank you for giving us the opportunity to do what we do in Hannibal. You truly are the wind beneath our wings.

There are so many others to thank: to Karen Martino, Ann Nagy and Bella Erakko-Taylor, thank you for your love and support, especially each time I put on the wig; to Rich Heiser and Terri McClain at *Hannibal* magazine, thank you for giving us such a wonderful platform to share our stories and for your support of the Hannibal History Museum; and to the James O'Donnell family, thank you for keeping the shamrocks green in Hannibal for more than a century and for supporting the Shindigs. We give a round of applause to all the members of the crazy RagTag Irish Band for drinking up all the Guinness and Jameson and giving us hours of joy in word and song. Thanks also go to Wesley Knapp, Chris Bobek, Arif Dagin, Stuart and Randy at the Parrot, Cindy Lovell, Sherri Steinmann, Mary Glenn Bowman, all the ladies of Beta Sigma Phi, Patrick Hyde, Joel and Faye Dant, Michael Gaines, Nora Creason, Stan and Cara Foster, Jack Klotz, Steve and Jackie Karlock and Mike and Elaine McFarlane for all your support of our efforts over the years. We also thank Dr. Kristen Iversen for leading the way.

Finally, to the Cline family: Keith, Christa, Shyenne and especially Monti. When we say we couldn't do it without you, we really mean it! You keep us afloat, sane, focused, neat, tidy and well fed, and you give us a break. You help us keep hope (and history) alive with your enthusiasm and devotion. We love you, and we're so grateful for all that you do.

Introduction

A Brief History of Molly's Hannibal

Hannibal, Missouri, hugs the western shore of the Mississippi River just one hundred miles north of St. Louis. Nicknamed the "Bluff City," the town is nestled in the valley between two great limestone bluffs, Cardiff Hill to the north and Lover's Leap to the south, both with elevations nearly three hundred feet above the river.

For centuries, Native Americans freely roamed the area of what is now northeastern Missouri. In late autumn, tribes of Fox and Illinois and Sauk (Sac) Indians would migrate to the region, traveling downriver from their northern farming territories to set up winter camps along the banks of the great river. Here the tribes would hunt and fish, canoe around the islands between the shores of the Mississippi and perform sacred rituals on the unusual geological formation that juts out over the river now known as Lover's Leap. No single tribe claimed the area as its own, but many would travel through the region as part of their nomadic traditions. The river was called *misi-ziibi* ("great river") by the Ojibwe (or Chippewa) tribe.

Beginning in the mid-seventeenth century, expeditions were regularly commissioned by both the French and Spanish governments to survey the great uncharted lands of North America cut in half by the dark, swirling waters of the Mississippi River. In 1800, just three years before Thomas Jefferson would purchase the territory from Napoleon, the Spanish government commissioned Don Antonio Soulard, a Frenchman working as the surveyor general for Spain, to formally survey and map the vast lands of Spanish Louisiana, which stretched from the Canadian border to the Gulf of Mexico and from the Rocky Mountains to the Mississippi River. As his published maps demonstrate, Soulard was obviously well versed in the history of ancient Rome, as several water features found during his exploration of what is now northeast Missouri bear names culled from popular Roman military leaders. Soulard named a small bay "Scipio" in honor of the Roman general who was victorious in the Second Punic War. A small river in the area was named "Fabius" for Fabius Maximus, the Roman general known for his skill in retreat. A short distance farther downstream, he came across another small tributary that wound its way through the valley between the twin bluffs, flowing west from the Mississippi, and he recorded the name of the creek as "Hannibal." (Hannibal, although defeated by Scipio in the Second Punic War, is still believed to be the greatest of all Carthaginian military commanders.) Thus, it was Soulard's map from 1800 that first bore the name Hannibal, marking the first recorded instance of the name's use in the area.

In 1816, a young man named Moses D. Bates arrived in St. Louis from Virginia to seek his fortune. One of Bates's first contracts was to build a home for General William Clark, who, after returning from his famous expedition with Meriwether Lewis, had been appointed governor of the Missouri Territory by Thomas Jefferson. During this time, Bates heard that William V. Rector, United States surveyor general, was planning to survey the northeast area of the Missouri Territory. He immediately secured an assignment to become part of the survey team as a chain carrier. The survey team commenced work in 1817 and continued into 1818. While working on the survey, Bates saw the potential of the land between the two great limestone bluffs as a settlement for fur trapping and trading with the native tribes in the region, and he began to dream of a bright new future.

After the survey was complete, Bates immediately engaged Jonathan Fleming, a friend and fellow carpenter, to travel upstream by keelboat to begin construction on the new settlement he envisioned. Bates selected what he believed to be a prime location near the banks of the Mississippi to make his camp; this small plot later became the southeast corner of Main and Bird Streets in downtown Hannibal.

Moses Bates continued to have business dealings in St. Louis and traveled up and down the Mississippi between the two settlements. It was during one of these business trips to St. Louis that Bates was introduced to Thompson Bird. Bird was the son of Abraham Bird, who happened to have been issued New Madrid Certificate #379, a land grant appropriated by the U.S. Congress that could be redeemed for 640 acres in any portion of Missouri not yet settled, compensation for the loss of his land during the New Madrid earthquake of 1811. The savvy Bates was able to convince Bird to redeem the certificate and stake a claim in the northeast portion of the territory, which would, of course, include Bates's two-cabin settlement near the river. Thompson Bird, having power of attorney and authority from his father, redeemed the New Madrid certificate for 640 acres covering parts of Sections 21, 28 and 29 in Township 57, Range 4. Once the claim was secured, he conveyed one-eighth interest in the land tract to Moses D. Bates and sold one-half interest to Elias Rector of St. Louis for $960. Thus, a new settlement was born.

The Steamboat Era Begins

Steamboats had been on the Mississippi as early as 1811 with the launch of the *Orleans* out of Pittsburgh, Pennsylvania. During that decade, there were about 20 steamboats navigating the Mississippi; by 1830, more than 1,200 were making the rounds between Minneapolis and New Orleans. On May 2, 1823, the first steamer to ascend the upper Mississippi left St. Louis. This was the *Virginia*, a side-wheeler 118 feet long by 22 feet across. This maiden voyage was headed by William Clark, who, after serving as governor of the Missouri Territory, had recently been named superintendent of Indian affairs by U.S. president James Monroe. Joining Clark was Lawrence Taliaferro, who served as the U.S. agent of Sioux affairs; Giacomo Constantine Betrami, an Italian explorer who kept a detailed journal of the excursion; Great Eagle, a Sauk tribal chief of the region; and Moses D. Bates.

This expedition must have had a profound impact on Moses Bates. Soon, yet another business venture began to take shape in Bates's entrepreneurial mind, and by 1825, Bates had achieved sufficient financial success through his various business interests to launch his most ambitious enterprise to date: the establishment of a steamboat line between St. Louis, Missouri, and Galena, Illinois. Galena, a small settlement some two hundred miles upstream from Hannibal and situated along the banks of the Fevre River that flowed east from the Mississippi, was booming after lead mines were discovered in the area in 1816. No doubt Bates heard about the extraordinary opportunities for shipping the ore down to southern refineries and was eager to expand the boundaries of his business dealings to take advantage of the prospect.

While on a business trip to St. Louis in the summer of 1825, Bates purchased a small side-wheeler, the *General Putnam*. The crew carried axes and would make frequent stops along the river to chop the wood necessary to make the steam that powered the vessel. Immediately, Bates and the crew of *General Putnam* began to make regular trips between the rich lead mines of Galena and the ever-growing port of St. Louis; on each trip, whether heading north or south, Bates would require that the ship pause for a short stop along the shores of Hannibal.

As other steamboats began to appear on the river, new settlers traveling along the Mississippi discovered Hannibal and soon began to gather on its shore. The census of 1830 reported thirty residents of the village. Construction was still made with rough-hewn logs, but a cluster of new cabins appeared in the valley between the bluffs and began to branch farther west away from the river. Moses Bates continued to contribute to the village's development, establishing a horse-powered mill for grinding flour and corn in 1827.

From a Village to a Town

As Moses Bates made his way between Galena and St. Louis, the fledgling community of Marion City was also beginning to grow just twelve miles upriver from Hannibal. Hailed as the future metropolis of the West, investors from the East, many of whom knew little to nothing of the topography of northeast Missouri, speculated on plots of land in what was to become Marion City in the hope of quick profits from new industries made possible from steamboats plying up and down the Mississippi. Carpenters and masons were sent to the area, and by 1835, the ambitious plans of the speculators were well under construction.

The spring of 1836 was cold and wet, with temperatures remaining cool throughout May. As the weather suddenly turned warm, the snows from the north began to rapidly melt and surge downstream. The sudden massive influx of melted snow flowed into the Mississippi and began to mix with northeast Missouri's unusually heavy late spring rains. Soon, residents noticed that the Mississippi River was slowly creeping into Marion City. Day by day, the shore would encroach a little farther. Eventually, the river overwhelmed the town; it was soon apparent to all that Marion City was situated in a floodplain.

By June 1836, during the height of the flooding, the entire town had become submerged. Muddy river waters and debris flowed into the second stories of some buildings. At the time, there was no way to forecast weather predictions or river flood stages, nor were there sufficient means of communication to warn those living along the banks of the Mississippi of the northern waters coming their way. The residents of Marion City were taken completely by surprise.

Then, as the floodwaters receded over the long, hot summer of 1836, malaria set in. Mosquitoes, unsanitary conditions, contaminated drinking water and the deep mud left behind by the retreating river brought sickness and death to Marion City. Those who could soon fled the town.

Some migrated twelve miles south to Hannibal, where, just three blocks west of the river, the landscape of the town sloped uphill to such a degree that "high ground" protected most residents from flooding. Hannibalians welcomed the Marion City refugees, providing shelter and sharing their food supplies. Hannibal saw its numbers swell from the thirty residents recorded in 1830 to nearly five hundred in 1837, in large part because of the failure of the community of Marion City. The carpenters, masons and plasterers who came to the area to build Marion City began to apply their skills toward the construction of Hannibal, and the riverside settlement began to grow.

A St. Louis newspaper, the *Daily Missouri Republican*, reported the plight of Marion City in "Removing a City," published on November 16, 1841:

> *The buildings of Marion City, on the Mississippi River, the same town in which so many eastern purchasers got their fingers burned a few years since, are being removed to Hannibal, a town some twelve miles below…When the buildings are removed to Hannibal they will be worth something, for there is no town on the Missouri side advancing more steadily and rapidly than this same place. Its business is already large in a commercial point of view, and within its limits is fast accumulating wealth, industry, population, and all the elements necessary to the creation of, in no distant day, a city.*

New industries began to spring up in the village of Hannibal. Mr. Amelung of Cincinnati began operation of the first pork-packing plant in 1837, located at the river's edge on Market Street (now Broadway). A second pork-packing plant, operated by Shields and Williams, also appeared near the levee in 1838. Pork packing would prove to be one of the most important industries in Hannibal throughout the nineteenth century. As Thomas H. Bacon reported in his 1905 publication *Mirror of Hannibal*, "The first marked prosperity arose with the pork and beef packing industry. As soon as the temperature sank enough, endless processions of hogs and cattle were headed for the tender mercies of the packing house…On arriving in town a farmer's first question was comprised in a single word, 'Wutsawgswuth.'"

During this time, the only reasonable method of transporting the hogs from farms to the packing plants was to drive them by foot. This meant that, on any given day, a large passel of hogs could be seen charging down Main Street toward the slaughterhouses situated near the levee. The squeals and bleating by themselves would produce quite a cacophony of sound; add to this the neigh of frightened horses, the bark of angry dogs and the pounding of hooves large and small on the packed dirt of Main Street, and it is easy to imagine the chaos this parade of livestock could cause. On rainy days, the mud would be mixed with pig droppings and other eliminations, exacerbating the situation. Surely, the sidewalks and storefronts would clear quickly if one heard the ill-fated hogs coming his way.

Regardless of its shortcomings, the pork-packing industry generated growth throughout the village. Thousands of barrels were required to pack the meat for shipment by steamboats churning up and down the river, and cooper shops multiplied to build the needed wooden barrels. Salt production was increased, boiled down from water gathered from the nearby, aptly named Salt River, and was used to aid in the preservation of the meat. Labor was needed for these operations, and advertisements announced that jobs were available in Hannibal. With population growth came the need for new housing, larger general stores, blacksmiths and other necessary services. The increased revenue generated by these new industries spurred further growth. The promise of opportunity and prosperity encouraged many new families to move into the area and call themselves Hannibalians. On March 1, 1839, after recording more than one thousand residents, Hannibal was officially incorporated into a town.

Antebellum Hannibal

Hannibal became a frequent stop for steamboats churning up and down the river, and each year, the boats arrived in greater numbers. Immigrants from all over the world arrived by steamboat to the shores of Hannibal. The growth of the new town was explosive.

Introduction

In November 1839, a family of modest means that included five children and one slave moved from Florida, Missouri, into the Virginia House, a small hotel on Hill Street just west of Main. The new owner of the Virginia House, John Marshall Clemens, had purchased the entire block of Hill Street where the Virginia House stood for $7,000 from Hannibalian "Big" Ira Stout. Clemens was enthusiastic about relocating his family to Hannibal and optimistic about the opportunities for prosperity in the booming river town. His second-youngest son, four-year-old Sammy Clemens, would one day become quite famous as the author and humorist Mark Twain.

In the 1840 census, Hannibal recorded 1,034 citizens. New buildings began to spring up on the riverfront. Brick buildings began populating Main Street—a drugstore, a general store, a tavern, a hotel. In October 1840, the First United Presbyterian Church began holding services in the first church building constructed in Hannibal on North Fourth Street between Bird and Hill Streets. Services at this church were attended by Jane Clemens and her young children, including ginger-haired Sammy.

The steamboats brought with them to Hannibal news, entertainment and needed goods. They left with products produced in Hannibal, shipping the bounty to distant shores to be sold. The paddle-wheelers would then come about, turning to make the trip back to Hannibal from the other direction with loads of cash. With the help of more than one thousand steamboats arriving on the levee each year, Hannibal was evolving from a

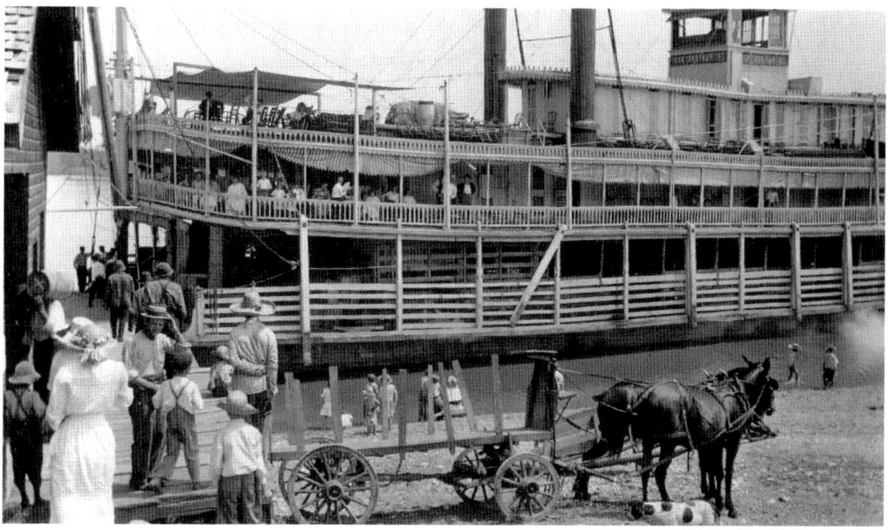

A "packet boat" docked at the Hannibal levee, circa 1870s. *Courtesy of Steve Chou.*

muddy, homespun pioneer village to a civilized, modern, mid-nineteenth-century town.

When Missouri was admitted to the Union as a state in 1821, slavery in the area expanded greatly. The Missouri Compromise of 1820 determined that Maine could join the Union as a "free state" (making the enslavement of blacks illegal) and, in an effort to balance power in the Senate, allowed that Missouri be deemed a "slave state." Many slaveholders from Virginia and Kentucky moved into the region in search of new land specifically because they could maintain ownership of their slaves. Because of this migration of slaveholders, northeastern Missouri was soon nicknamed "Little Dixie" because of the volume of southerners who poured into the state after 1820.

Despite the movement toward "civilization," it was not a happy-go-lucky existence for everyone in Hannibal. The black population of the town, whether slave or free, black or mulatto, was under constant watch, never allowed the opportunities of its white counterparts. When Hannibal was incorporated in 1839, one of the first acts of the new Hannibal Board of Trustees was "An Ordinance Respecting Slaves, Free Negroes, or Mulattoes," adopted just nineteen days after the board was first named. The ordinance prohibited certain activities by blacks and outlined the punishment of both the black residents who broke the rules and whites who enabled them. There were eight sections adopted in the ordinance, covering everything from the "wanton galloping of a horse through town by a Negro" to the "unlawful gathering of Negroes in groups greater than five."

Not everyone in Missouri was supportive of slavery, however. Abolitionists were present throughout the state, particularly along the western shores of the Mississippi to aid runaway slaves trying to get across the river into the free state of Illinois. Hannibal, in particular, became one of those gateways to freedom; Quincy, Illinois, just twenty miles upstream, was a major stop for runaway slaves traveling along the Underground Railroad.

On February 24, 1845, Hannibal was incorporated as a city, having been granted a charter by the State of Missouri after reaching a population of more than 1,500 souls. Civic leadership in Hannibal began to have a major impact on the new city's future. In 1846, a public meeting was held in the office of Judge John Marshall Clemens. About a dozen people attended the meeting to discuss an exciting new plan for the city of Hannibal: the establishment of the Hannibal & St. Joseph Railroad. The group adopted the plan and asked Robert F. Lakenan, secretary of the committee, to prepare the charter immediately for presentation to the Missouri legislature.

Although the small group had no experience and little knowledge of what was involved in building a railroad, it did have the foresight to know the impact the railway would have on the future of Hannibal. A rail line that cut directly across the state to the western city of St. Joseph would provide a route to ship Hannibal goods to markets in the developing West, possibly equaling the volume of goods currently being sent south by steamboat. It would take more than twelve years before the line was completed, but the small group of men from Hannibal, including the town's justice of the peace, was instrumental in securing a major transportation pipeline that would have a profound impact on Hannibal for more than a century.

By 1847, flour production had become big business in the area, with more than 110,000 bushels of wheat brought to Hannibal for milling and export that year. Other industries were thriving as well. Two hundred tons of hemp were used annually in Hannibal's ropewalks, with rope being a prime product manufactured in town. John Garth, who moved to Hannibal with his family in 1844, began a tobacco processing business and produced cigars and plug and chewing tobacco, exporting more than 500,000 pounds of products per year from his new facility. According to the February 25, 1847 edition of the *Hannibal Gazette*, a total of more than $1.2 million of goods had been produced in Hannibal the previous year.

The city was now home to twenty carpenters, fifteen physicians, fourteen wholesale and retail general stores, twelve attorneys, eight tailors, six brickyards, six blacksmiths, five cabinetmakers and undertakers, three hotels, three sawmills (one of them powered by steam), three saddle shops, two druggists, two watchmakers, two livery stables, a tan yard and a steam distillery. Amos and Brison Stillwell, who came to Hannibal in 1845, engaged in a new milling business at the mouth of Bear Creek. The Stillwells would also be involved in pork packing. Three hundred men were employed in the various pork-packing facilities along the levee, where, during a six-month period in 1847, 13,000 hogs and 4,500 hundred cattle were driven down Main Street to be slaughtered.

In contrast to the advancement of Hannibal's white citizens, both enslaved and free blacks continued to be oppressed. In Marion County, whose largest town was Hannibal, more than 2,300 slaves were kept. In addition, 42 "free" blacks were in residence, former slaves who were either able to purchase their freedom or were declared free in the last will and testaments of their now-deceased owners. These so-called free blacks were required to post bond and register with the city or county where they lived and were banned from most jobs, relegating them to work as sharecroppers or domestics right alongside slaves.

Another dichotomy of black and white culture in Hannibal could be seen in education. White children were being taught in both public and private schools in Hannibal, including the Hannibal Academy and Mary Newcomb's school in the basement of the Presbyterian church, where Sam Clemens was sometimes a student. However, in 1847, the Missouri legislature passed a law forbidding the "teaching of Negroes or mulattoes, with the penalty of a $500 fine or six months' imprisonment." The fear was that, if taught to read and write, blacks might be influenced by abolition literature smuggled into the community and would encourage one another to rise up in rebellion. While many in Hannibal supported this view, the city continued to see its fair share of abolitionists as well. As the question of slavery became more intense across the nation, tensions in town would also rise between the two factions.

The Lure of Riches in Western Mines

On January 24, 1848, James Wilson Marshall, originally from Platte County, Missouri, stumbled across gold nuggets in the water of his sawmill near the confluence of the American and Sacramento Rivers in California. Employees of the sawmill and adjacent businesses quickly began to search the area and also discovered gold. Soon, word spread throughout California and the Oregon Territories—and thus, the California Gold Rush began.

It took quite a while for the news to arrive on the shores of Hannibal. When the discovery of gold in California was first reported, some Hannibalians were skeptical of what seemed like a "get rich quick" scheme. However, when President James Polk spoke of the discovery in his message to Congress in December 1848, people all over the United States began to dream of the riches that were waiting for them out west. Gold rush fever began to grip the town of Hannibal.

On December 7, 1848, the *Hannibal Journal* reported that a small group of Missouri men had returned to St. Joseph from California with a large quantity of gold dust, and a local Hannibal jeweler had obtained two samples of the gold dust for locals to examine. An editorial published on December 29, 1848, spoke of "Gold Fever." One week later, on January 4, the *Journal* quoted a man from St. Louis who claimed to have made the trip from California back to Independence, Missouri, in only one hundred days by oxcart. Tilden Selmes, a merchant whose warehouse was located on the northeast corner of Main and Hill Streets, began a series of advertisements in the *Journal* proclaiming, "Ho! For California!" that offered a list of items one would require to make the trip and exhorted his expertise in furnishing said supplies for the adventure. Gold rushers from the East began arriving in Hannibal by steamboat, stopping to gather supplies on their way west to St. Joseph, Missouri and beyond. Their enthusiasm whipped some local residents into a frenzy of excitement, and the town was abuzz with reports of men banding together and preparing for their trip.

This would not be the last time that rumors of great opportunities in the West would spur Hannibalians to migrate toward a brighter future.

Prologue

Lifeboat No. 6

As she felt the oars softly penetrate the water alongside her, black as ink, and she stared up into the magnificent star-filled sky, memories came to her, fleeting glimpses of the past that she hadn't recalled in many years. The sound of the ocean as it lapped against the side of the small dinghy was the same sound the Mississippi River's current would make as it came ashore. The pungent smell of the coal smoke emanating from the ship's boilers was reminiscent of her father's oil-stained clothes as he came through the front door of their small cottage after a long day's work. The screech of metal as *Titanic* twisted and splintered before disappearing into the cold North Atlantic sounded like the saw blades of the old lumber mills cutting through dense timbers. In the silence that followed, as long hours dragged on seemingly without end, the memories came flooding back.

Margaret was overwhelmingly grateful that Helen had stayed behind in Paris. Her daughter, so beautiful at the age of twenty-three, with long auburn hair and flawless alabaster skin, begged her mother to allow her to stay and enjoy the company of friends for a few weeks longer before making the long voyage back to the shores of America. Reluctantly, Margaret acquiesced. She had to remind herself at times that Helen was older now than Margaret had been when *her* mother allowed her to step onto the train at Union Depot, bound for Colorado, leaving home for the first time.

Margaret realized that it was possible she was being too dramatic when she suddenly insisted on returning to the States after receiving the telegram notifying her of her grandson's illness, but she had yet to lay eyes on her first grandchild, only five months old, and she felt it necessary to abandon the remaining portion of her European vacation with Helen and the Astors and return to Missouri in order to help care for the child. She had asked John Astor to advise her on the quickest way back to the States. He had told her she was "in luck" because he and his wife, Madeline, had booked their return passage on the maiden voyage of a new ocean liner, the finest in the world. It was the next ship leaving for America, and he would be pleased to assist her in securing two first-class tickets. Margaret remembered that she had told John that it was not necessary for Helen to accompany her, so only one ticket was required. Besides, Margaret had decided that as she would make her way back west, she would take a few days to stop in Hannibal for a visit. Helen didn't appreciate Hannibal the way Margaret did.

Hannibal. Such a small corner of the world, made to seem even more so since Margaret had explored many exotic locales throughout Europe and Asia. But there was no place like home, no place that she could let down her guard, be with those who knew her before she was famous (or infamous, as some believed), knew her as a child and young lady and understood where she had come from and what had made her who she was. There was comfort in being with like-minded folk, comfort in slipping back into familiar speech patterns and social customs from which you'd grown accustomed as a child. Although her wanderlust kept her continually on the move, Margaret always looked forward to her return trips home to Hannibal.

Regardless of what J.J. said about her being raised with "hoggs," Margaret was proud to be from Hannibal. She recalled her childhood there just as fondly as Mark Twain had, and she was proud, too, that the world had also fallen in love with Hannibal after reading *The Adventures of Tom Sawyer*. She was proud of her Irish roots and Catholic faith and knew that who she'd become—the beliefs central to her core being—came from her experiences growing up in Hannibal.

Suddenly, Margaret snapped back to the present. The oars were as heavy as lead, her arms even heavier, yet she knew her survival, and the survival of those around her, depended on her ability to keep moving, to keep herself warm, to endure this unfathomable ordeal. They were the lucky ones, the one-third who made it onto the lifeboats, the persons selected by a higher power to be given the chance to continue their lives. Margaret mustered her strength and kept on rowing.

Prologue

The burden of that privilege, of finding a way to live the remainder of your life in a manner that was worthy of the gift of extra time, would drive Margaret to achieve great things. It would be unfortunate that the world, particularly the press, would misunderstand her motivation for doing so. It had nothing to do with Margaret wanting to get her name in the papers for self-promotion—ironically, the reason her name appeared in newspapers was because the reporters, who apparently had nothing more interesting to write about than what she was up to, sought her out and used her celebrity to sell their newspapers. Even Margaret's own children would not understand why she pushed herself so hard and why she sacrificed everything for the causes she championed, even at the risk of losing her family. No, it wasn't the need for attention. Truth be told, Margaret, whether consciously or otherwise, pushed herself to achieve her lofty goals purely to conquer the deep-seated feeling that to do otherwise would mean that she hadn't deserved the extra time she had been given, that she hadn't deserved to survive.

But survive she did. It was in her blood, this will to survive. It stemmed from an inner strength Margaret had inherited from both of her "Famine Irish" parents.

Part I

John Tobin's Journey

Situated in a lush, green valley between steep hills that lead downward to the shores of the Blackwater River, one finds the picturesque town of Fermoy. This small parish of County Cork, Ireland, named for the Cistercian abbey founded there by Benedictine monks in the twelfth century, saw its population grow by one with the birth of John Tobin in 1823.

John entered into a world where life was exceedingly hard for the residents of Ireland. Penal laws enacted in the 1600s as a means to force Irish Catholics to accept the reformed Christian faith of the Anglican Church of England prevented Catholics from owning land, voting, holding public office or obtaining any sort of education. Although many of the penal laws were reformed by 1829, Catholics, who comprised nearly 80 percent of the Irish population, owned less than 5 percent of the land. A vast majority of the Irish worked as tenant farmers on small patches of land leased to them by their English landlords. These farms, most less than fifteen acres, forced Ireland and its peasantry into a monoculture; the plots of land were so small that livestock could not be raised, and only potatoes, which could be grown abundantly and in less favorable soil, would yield enough food to feed their families. The rights to tend these small farms meant the difference between life and death for the impoverished Irish in the early nineteenth century.

While the British held all of Ireland under imperial rule, the 9,500 residents who resided in Fermoy at the time of John Tobin's birth suffered more than most. A major barracks for the British army had been constructed in Fermoy in 1797, and by 1830, when young John Tobin was just seven years old, the encampment had grown to become the largest British military establishment on the island of Ireland. The Irish of Fermoy were under constant surveillance by the military, and tensions ran high.

In a move that would further complicate life for the Irish, the New Poor Law Amendment Act was passed in 1834 by the British Parliament to reform the United Kingdom's poverty relief system, replacing earlier legislation based on the Poor Law Act of 1601. The new act called for parishes to be joined together into poor law unions so that relief could be provided more efficiently. Each designated union was instructed to build a workhouse as a place where those unable to support themselves could find shelter, food and employment.

However, the new poor law union workhouses were not designed to help the poor; they were designed to punish them. According to the act, the workhouse must meet the principles of "Less Eligibility," which mandated that working conditions in the workhouse had to be worse than the worst job possible outside the workhouse. This principle existed to deter able-bodied people from claiming relief rather than working. Life in a workhouse was intended to be harsh to ensure that only the truly destitute would apply; it was designed to humiliate the impoverished Irish into work.

The Fermoy Poor Law Union was formally declared on February 23, 1839, linking nearby towns together and establishing a workhouse in Fermoy. An existing barracks building in the British army's complex was adapted and expanded into a workhouse to accommodate up to nine hundred of the impoverished Irish of the region. The first admissions were received at the workhouse on July 6, 1841.

Conditions in the Fermoy workhouse were extraordinarily severe. Those interred in the workhouse were segregated into four divisions: the elderly and infirm, children, able-bodied men and able-bodied women. One reason for separating the sexes was based on a principle outlined in a widely read treatise of the time by the Anglican reverend Thomas Robert Malthus that stated, "The power of population is indefinitely greater than the power in the earth to produce subsistence for man." Malthus argued that two factors were required to hold populations in check so as to not overburden the earth's capability to provide adequate food supplies: positive checks, such as famine, war and disease, and preventive checks, such as lowering the birth rate. He proposed the gradual abolition of poor laws by gradually reducing the number of persons qualifying for relief; by segregating the sexes in workhouses, the number of those born into poverty could be controlled and, it was hoped, eventually eliminated.

Although most residents of Fermoy were able to avoid the workhouse when it was first constructed, soon the situation worsened further. Just four years later, in 1845, *an Gorta Mór* ("The Great Hunger") began. The disease *Phytophthorae infestans*, commonly known as blight, attacked the Irish potato crop in 1844. By the summer of 1845, it had spread across Europe into England, France, Germany, Belgium and Holland. Crop losses that year were as high as half of cultivated acreage; the next growing season, three-fourths of the harvest was lost to blight.

During the first year of the famine, the Fermoy workhouse was expanded to hold additional inmates, but soon the workhouse was overcome by the influx of the starving Irish. Whether sick or healthy, as people were admitted to the workhouse, they were crowded into wards; on one occasion, thirty children suffering disease and hunger were found occupying just three beds in the Fermoy workhouse.

A New Life in America

Thus the great Irish Diaspora began. The Irish began to flee their homeland for a better life in England, Scotland, Canada, Australia or the United States, and by 1860, nearly 2 million Irish had reached the shores of America. The journey across the sea was horrific, as hordes were packed into vessels referred to as "coffin ships," most of which were unseaworthy, overcrowded and lacking sufficient provisions of drinking water, food or sanitation. Many ships would be lost at sea when overwhelmed by storms. Of those who attempted the month-long journey, roughly 20 percent of the passengers would not survive the trip, dying from disease and hunger. It is not known when John Tobin was able to escape the horrific conditions of life in his hometown, but at some point, he said goodbye to his beloved Ireland and made the treacherous journey across the Atlantic in order to begin a new life in America.

During this same period, the Germans also began to immigrate en masse to America. More than 1 million Germans came in the 1850s, some seeking religious freedom; many, though, were inspired by a bestselling book published in 1829 by Gottfried Duden, *Bericht über Eine Reise Nach den Westlichen Staaten Nordamerika's* (*Report of a Journey to the Western States of North America*). Duden, who had established a farm on the banks of the Missouri River near what is now Washington, Missouri, compared the Missouri River to the Rhine in Germany and waxed poetically about the climate, soil conditions and culture of Missouri. His book inspired millions of Germans to immigrate to America and tens of thousands to settle in Missouri.

In contrast to the Irish, the Germans arrived in America healthy and happy. Many Germans had brought with them the financial means to start a business or purchase land and were well equipped with the education and experience to succeed in the New World. The Irish, less concerned with the adventure of a new land but simply fighting to survive, came to America with little or no money or education and were starving and diseased. Their only option was to populate the city in which they arrived and begin to work in any job available to them. It is a testament to their fortitude that so many Irish survived their harrowing sea voyage, worked their way out of the inner-city slums and earned the resources necessary to begin to migrate westward.

Many of the ships bringing the Irish famine immigrants to North America landed along the shores of Canada, some pulling into the port of St. John, New Brunswick. John Tobin, traveling from Ireland to the New World with one of his uncles, worked his way from Canada southward, eventually settling in the area of what is now Harpers Ferry, West Virginia, with other members of the Tobin family. As immigrants from around the world spread out across America, often they would choose to begin their new life in a region whose topography and climate resembled their native land; Harpers Ferry, founded at the confluence of the Shenandoah and Potomac Rivers—with large, rolling hills all around—must have reminded the Tobin clan of their home in Fermoy and would have been a familiar and comfortable place for them to begin anew. It was here where John married his first wife, Catherine Degott. The couple welcomed a daughter, Catherine "Katie" Bridget Tobin, who was born on June 14, 1857.

At the time the Tobin family lived in Harpers Ferry, the state of Virginia was at the forefront of tensions over slavery. Very much a slave state, Virginia did not have the kind of organized antislavery movements that were seen in the border states of Kentucky, Maryland and Delaware. However, in communities populated by immigrant settlers such as the Germans and Irish, antislavery sentiment was dominant. Harpers Ferry, only forty-five miles from the border of the free state of Pennsylvania, was a likely place for runaway slaves to make their way through the Underground Railroad. Of course, in October 1859, just two years after Katie was born, Harpers Ferry was made famous when John Brown led his followers on a raid of the United States Arsenal in an unsuccessful effort to arm rebellious slaves in the area. Family lore has it that John Tobin participated in abolitionist activities while living in Virginia. One can imagine that John, who witnessed the subjugation of his fellow Irishmen at the hands of the British, would have been sympathetic to the plight of the enslaved black population of the United States.

Sometime in 1858 or 1859, John's young wife, Catherine, passed away, leaving him a widower with their small daughter, Katie. Many factors might have contributed to John's decision to pull up stakes and take his daughter westward to begin a new chapter of their lives. Perhaps it was an attempt to leave behind the painful memories of Catherine's passing or the tensions in Virginia as the threat of civil war loomed over the region or the lure of the expansion of the railroads leading to the riches of western gold and silver mines; for whatever personal reasons John Tobin may have had, he and young Katie left Virginia. In the United States Census of 1860, John Tobin is found living in Hannibal, Missouri.

Migration to Missouri

By 1860, Missouri had become the destination for hundreds of thousands of immigrants. The 1860 census of St. Louis, then the fourth-largest city in America, revealed the largest foreign-born population in the country: half of the city's residents were Germans, and one-third were Irish. Many Germans would follow Duden's advice and farm the rich lands of middle Missouri, but the Irish mostly stayed in the cities. In Ireland, they had been used to small farms with neighbors close by, living in a community that was very social with gatherings, music, visits to local pubs, weddings, wakes and other events. In Missouri, they found vast lands with large farms, their nearest neighbors too far away to visit regularly, and the Irish culture did not take well to the isolation of the rural Missouri countryside. Further, larger American towns and cities gave the Irish new freedoms that they were not able to enjoy in their homeland, including religious freedom, voting rights, the opportunity to hold public office and free presses—rights that the Irish were eager to exercise.

To trace the steps of the Irish moving away from America's eastern cities in the mid-1800s, one need only follow the trails of the railroads being built during this time. While many Irish contributed to the actual construction

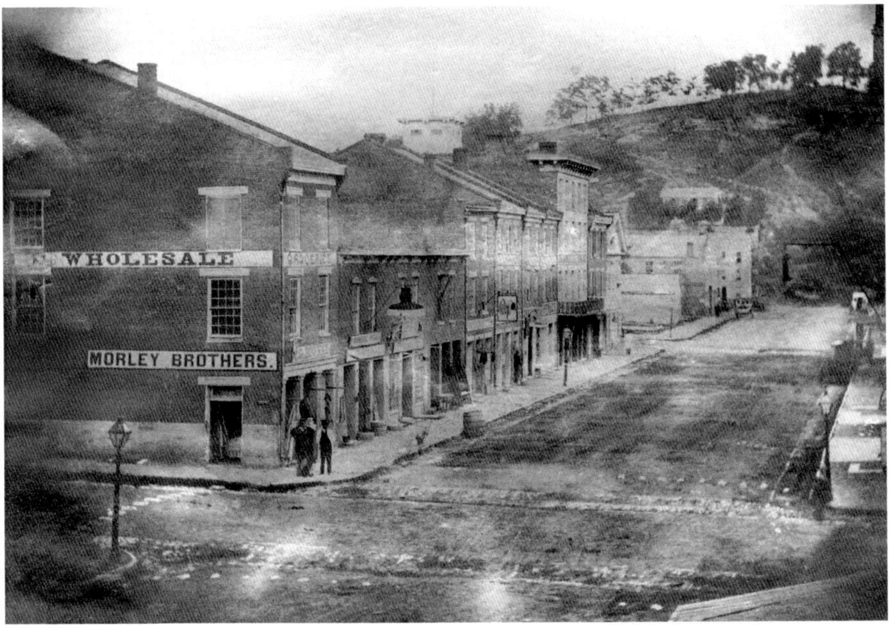

Main Street in Hannibal, looking north from the intersection of Bird Street, circa 1860s. *Courtesy of Steve Chou.*

of the railroads, others simply boarded these trains and congregated in the villages and towns where the trains made stops. Thus, when construction of the Hannibal & St. Joseph Railroad commenced in the early 1850s, the population of Hannibal's Irish community began to grow. According to census records, by 1870 there were 879 persons living in Marion County who were foreign-born Irish; if American-born descendants of the Irish immigrants were included, the total "Irish" population would have been near 3,000, or one-third of all Hannibal residents.

Upon his arrival in Hannibal, John Tobin found himself in familiar territory: a picturesque small town nestled in a valley between two great bluffs, lush with green and bordered by a mighty river. As did Harpers Ferry, Hannibal would have reminded him of his boyhood in Fermoy, Ireland, along the shores of the Blackwater River. Because of its familiar landscape, and the opportunity to prosper in this rapidly growing river town with its new railroad, it is no surprise that Hannibal is where John and young Katie settled in to begin the next chapter of their lives.

The Irish in Hannibal were predominantly Catholic. The first organized Catholic masses in Hannibal were celebrated by Reverend Father Patrick

Fleming in 1851 with only a handful of families in attendance. By 1859, construction of the first Church of the Immaculate Conception at 512 Church Street had been completed under the supervision of Reverend Father James Murphy, and the parish grew to 1,500 members.

The church was the center of social life for the tight-knit community of Hannibal's Irish. It was at an Immaculate Conception church picnic that John Tobin met his future wife, Johanna Collins. Johanna, also born in Ireland, had immigrated to America as a young girl and was raised in Pennsylvania. She, too, had been previously married; while living with her husband, Andreas Redner, in Davenport, Iowa, the couple welcomed the birth of their daughter, Mary Ann, born on January 1, 1856. Sadly, Johanna would soon grieve the death of her husband, and the young widow, along with little Mary Ann, somehow made her way to Hannibal. Upon their subsequent introduction and courtship, and not long after the dedication of the recently constructed Immaculate Conception church, John and Johanna were married at the altar of the new church by Father Murphy.

Although stories abound of businesses displaying signs reading, "Help Wanted: Irish Not Need Apply," these were probably found much more frequently in East Coast cities such as Boston and New York than in Missouri. According to Hannibal city directories from the 1850s and '60s, the Irish, although scattered throughout Hannibal, seemed to congregate their homes in two main areas, close to their employers: along Palmyra Avenue (now called Mark Twain Avenue), in proximity to the Hannibal Gas, Light and Coke Company and the D.J. Garth & Brothers Tobacco Company, and throughout the south side of Hannibal near the rail yards and lumberyards. These industries would employ scores of Irish as laborers, some able to work their way into supervisory and management positions. After their marriage, John and Johanna Tobin made their home in a modest, three-room cottage on the slope of Denkler's Alley in a small enclave of Irish residences overlooking Palmyra Avenue. John eventually found work as a laborer at the nearby Hannibal Gas, Light and Coke Company, where he would serve for the next twenty years.

Hannibal city directories also show that while a majority of the town's Irish were employed as laborers, others served in professions such as butchers, printers, sales clerks, firemen, shoemakers and tailors. A few of the early Irish who settled in Hannibal had the means to start their own businesses. The *Polk's Hannibal City Directory* of 1859 records the first known listing for Hibernia House, a boardinghouse located on Bird between Main Street and the levee under the proprietorship of Dennis O'Grady. *Hibernia* is the

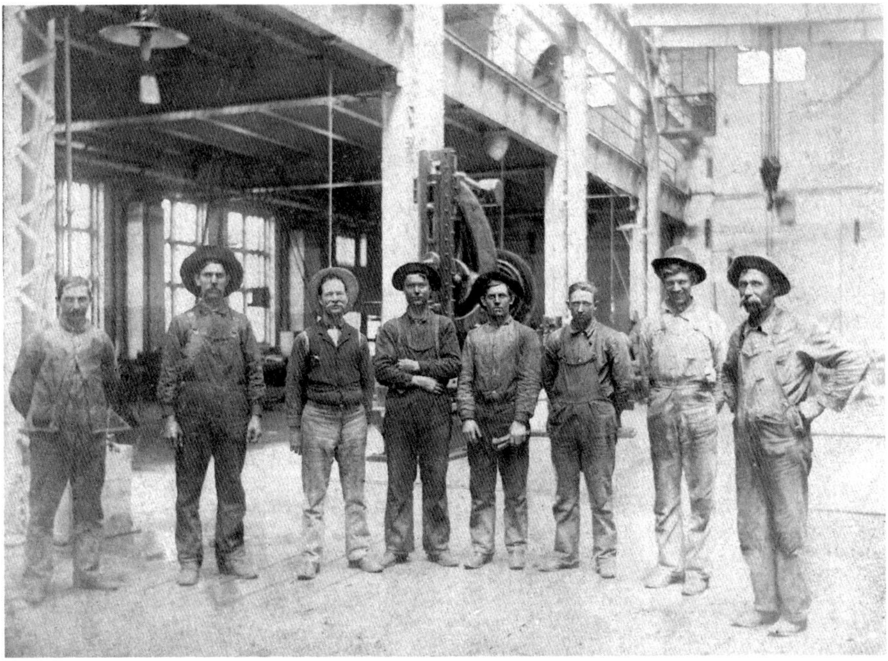

Railroad workmen stand inside one of Hannibal's earliest roundhouses, located just south of downtown Hannibal. *Courtesy of Steve Chou.*

classical Latin term for the island of Ireland; by its name, it is clear that this boardinghouse was intended to provide shelter and a social gathering place for the Irish in Hannibal. The popularity of Hibernia House is evident, as its listing can be found in directories throughout the 1870s.

The Civil War in Hannibal

As John and Johanna Tobin and their daughters, Katie and Mary Ann, began their new life together, the town around them, truly the *country* around them, was rapidly changing. For decades, it had been widely accepted throughout northeast Missouri's Little Dixie that slaveholding was a lawful practice, one that residents were obliged to defend. Usually, it was only the most radical antislavery abolitionists, those who believed God's law rose above the laws of man, who tried to interfere; each time they would stage some public display

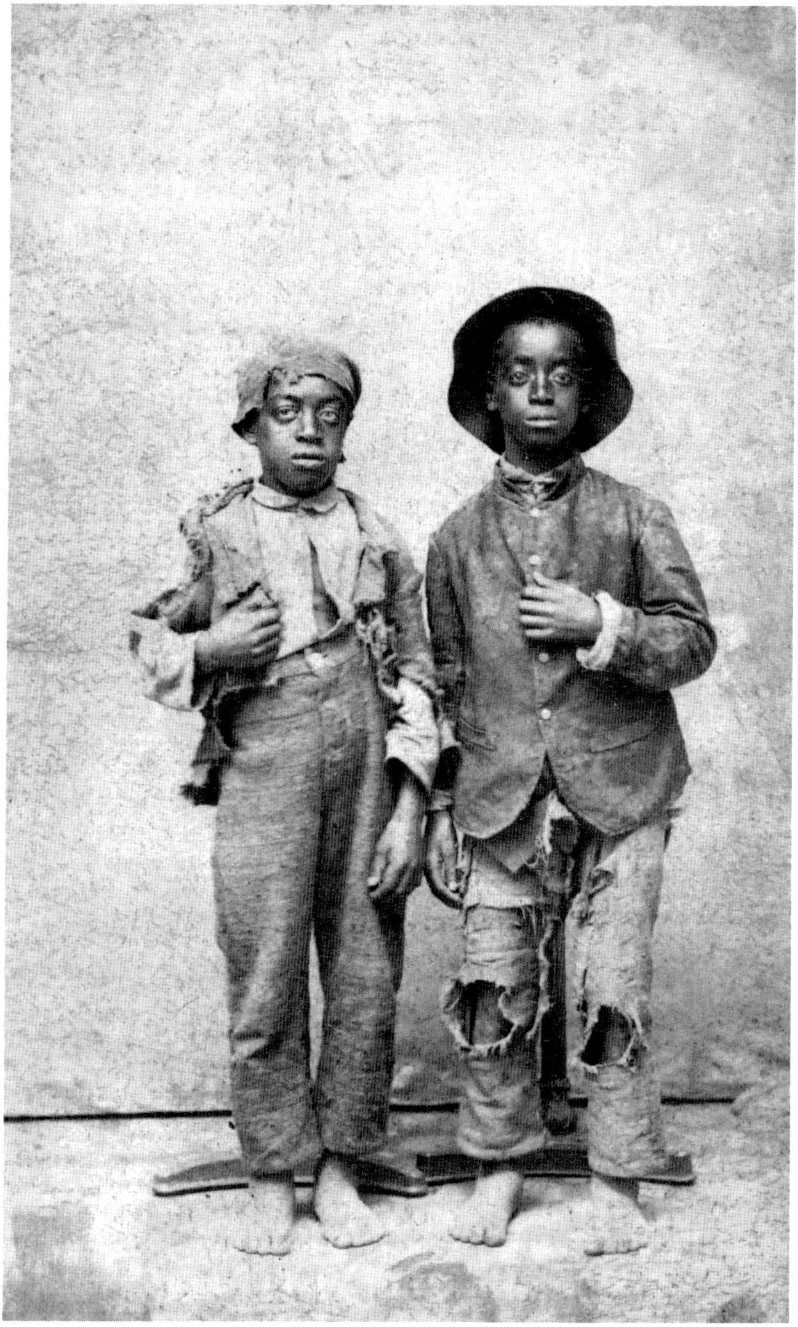

Two young black boys photographed in a Hannibal studio during the Civil War. The issue of slavery had fractured the community into myriad factions leading up to the war. *Courtesy of the Library of Congress.*

against slavery, however, the community would either drive them out of town or back underground. In northeast Missouri, even those who disagreed with slavery kept their opinions to themselves. For many years, slavery was the issue in Hannibal that people simply didn't talk about.

As war approached, however, Hannibal grew more and more deeply divided. Abolitionists in Hannibal, who had been working clandestinely for many years to smuggle runaway slaves across the Mississippi into free Illinois, became more emboldened to speak out. This faction, when combined with the influx of German and Irish immigrants who arrived in Hannibal in the late 1850s who were largely sympathetic to antislavery opinions, made up a much larger percentage of Hannibal's population than in previous decades. Although many Hannibal residents were southerners who had migrated to northeast Missouri with their slaves and continued to support the Confederacy, an almost equal number of Unionists were also present who were now outwardly vocal in their opposition. Hannibal became a border town in a border state, equally divided between Union and Confederate.

The Hannibal & St. Joseph Railroad was another major factor in Hannibal's civil war. The largest shareholders of the rail line were Boston-based Unionists; for businessmen in Hannibal, to support the Confederacy and cut ties with the Union would mean losing the railway and, with it, access to Northern investment, raw materials and markets, all of which had defined and supported the city's success. Slaveholders also understood the ramifications of this choice, as the local economy did not function in a way that would simply blend in with the South if secession occurred. Even the most ardent slaveholders in Missouri did not support secession and agreed that Missouri should remain a neutral border state.

Federal land grants provided to the Hannibal & St. Joseph Railroad Company in the early 1850s for the railway's construction had come with conditions, one of them being the right to transport Federal (Union) troops without restriction. Thus, from the first day of the Civil War, the railway was a vital asset to the Union and, therefore, a major target for destruction by the Confederacy. Bushwhackers were blamed for early attacks on trains running along the Hannibal & St. Joseph line through the spring and summer of 1861; they fired blindly into cars suspected of carrying Federal troops, even when the cars were mainly filled with civilian passengers. In addition, bushwhackers and volunteer Confederate troops were encouraged to sabotage the railways themselves. Tracks were taken apart or rail beds damaged, and base supports of trestle bridges were cut or burned surreptitiously. In the latter instance, a train would be driven onto the bridge before an engineer realized that it had

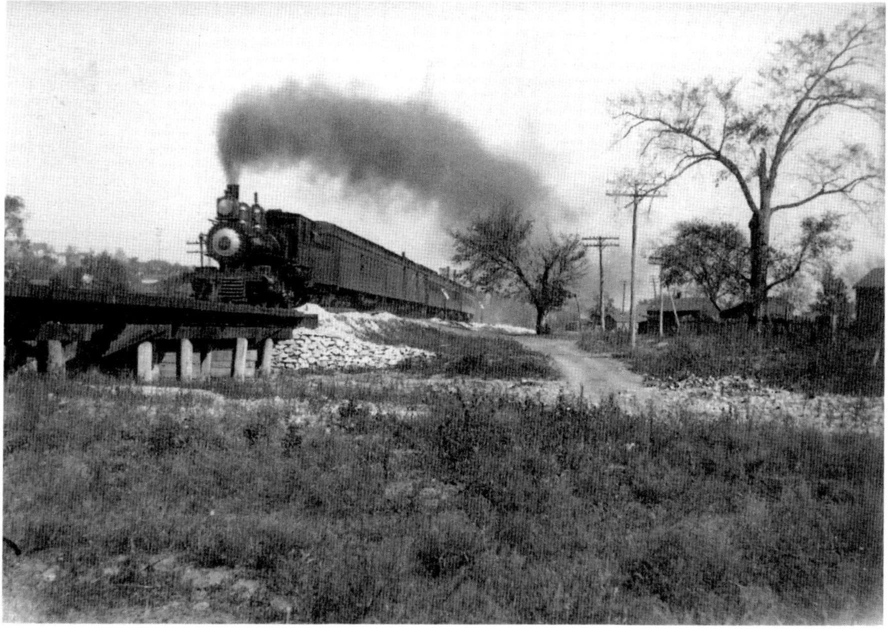

The Hannibal & St. Joseph Railroad, the first railroad to cross the state of Missouri and link the Mississippi and Missouri Rivers in 1859, created an economic boon for Hannibal. *Courtesy of Steve Chou.*

been compromised. On September 3, 1861, an act of sabotage culminated with a westbound train driving off a collapsing Platte Bridge outside Kansas City, killing twenty and injuring over one hundred people.

In Missouri, both the Union and Confederate governments called for residents to establish volunteer militias to defend their interests. According to family accounts, John Tobin joined one of these local Union regiments. From his brigade headquarters in Quincy, Illinois, Major General John C. Frémont, U.S. Army, reported on July 27, 1861, "I hold Hannibal with one company of Palmer's Fourteenth Illinois and three ill-disciplined companies of home guards." It is possible that John Tobin served in this capacity as a member of one of Hannibal's "Home Guard" details (which later became Company I, Tenth Missouri Infantry), or he may have been part of a unit of local volunteers assigned to protect the railroad line.

In order to defend the Hannibal & St. Joseph Railroad and keep steamboat traffic under control on the Mississippi, Union troops occupied Hannibal throughout the war. The town was placed under martial law, and no one could enter or exit the city limits without a pass. In an obvious show of force, on June 18, 1861, Colonel R.F. Smith and his Sixteenth Illinois Infantry planted their largest cannon, nicknamed "Black Betty," high atop Lover's Leap, not only to have the best shot from the high ground but also as a conspicuous visual demonstration of their firepower. They occupied integral buildings to ensure that the day-to-day business of Hannibal was not disrupted. Union control of the state also took precedence over resolving slavery status until the outcome of the war became more obvious; even after the Emancipation Proclamation was issued in 1863, any runaway slaves found by Federal troops were returned to their masters, as Missouri would not officially approve emancipation until January 1865. In contrast, however, by mid-1863, free black men in and around Hannibal (and probably a few who convinced recruiters that they were free) were recruited for the Union and shipped off to join the Massachusetts Fifty-fifth Volunteer Regiment, a sister regiment to Robert Gould Shaw's Fifty-fourth, which sent the first predominantly black troops into battle (commemorated in the 1989 film *Glory*). Three members of the Massachusetts Fifty-fifth are interred at Hannibal's Old Baptist Cemetery today, along with many others who served as members of U.S. and Missouri Colored Infantry Divisions.

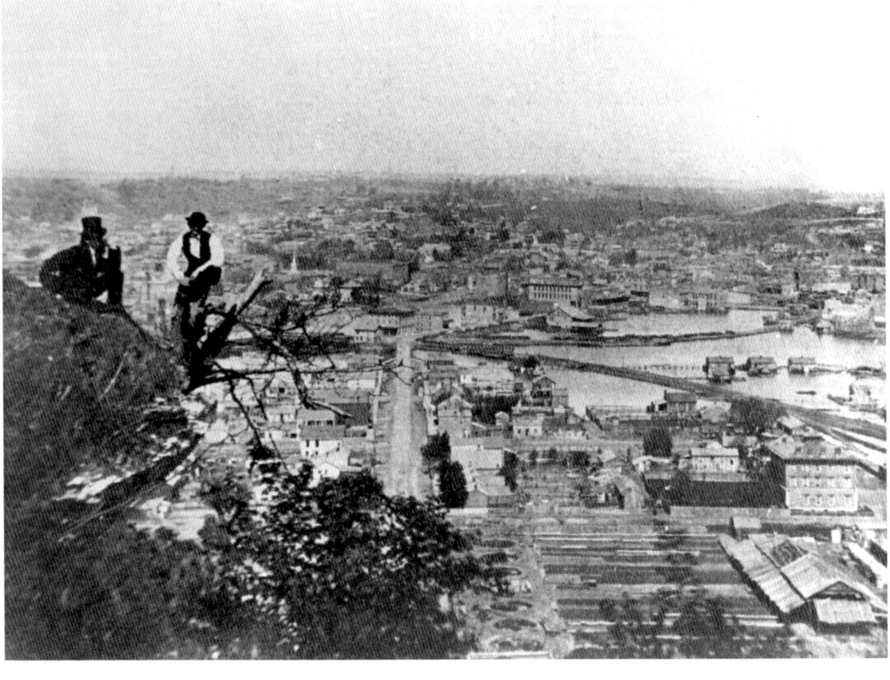

Two men pose on Lover's Leap, with Hannibal's downtown railroad and industrial districts visible below, circa 1880s. *Courtesy of Steve Chou.*

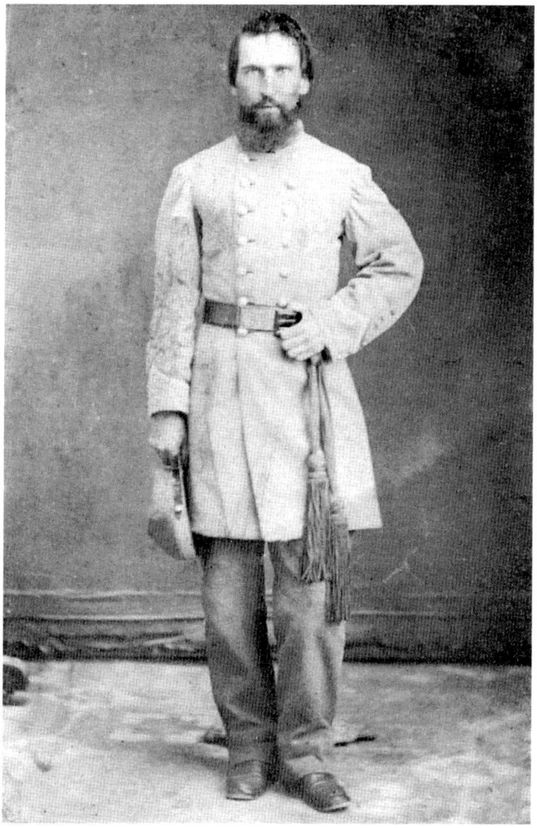

Confederate major George W. Bates of Hannibal, one of the sons of Hannibal founder Moses D. Bates. Northeast Missouri had been primarily settled by Confederate-sympathizing white Southerners and their slaves before the influx of immigrants and Northerners in the railroading era. *Courtesy of Steve Chou.*

For four long years, divided loyalties within the city of Hannibal created unrest and suspicion. Union and Confederate "eyes" were everywhere, and there were innumerable incidents reported where Union forces, Confederate soldiers or Confederate-supporting bushwhackers would attack, rob, violate or humiliate unarmed citizens. Although many of the reports against the Federal troops came from Confederate-sympathizing newspapers, even the superintendent of the Hannibal & St. Joseph, the staunchly Unionist J.T.K. Hayward, sent dispatches back east warning that the behavior and activities of the Union troops risked turning the citizens of Hannibal against the government. Although few sites in Missouri experienced full-fledged battles during the Civil War, the state was riddled with conflicts considered skirmishes—as many as 1,600 of them during the length of the war, according to some historians.

The Civil War brought Hannibal's prewar prosperity to a halt. Over the course of the war, the population dropped from ten thousand to less than six thousand as men were killed in service and families fled to escape the tension in town. Most industries in Hannibal converted to supporting the war effort and relied on government contracts for their revenues, which caused some prosperous businessmen to see their fortunes dwindle; only a few were able to maintain or increase their holdings through lucrative dealings with the

Unionists. Crops and grocery warehouses were often either confiscated by Union troops or raided by Confederate bushwhackers. The Hannibal & St. Joseph Railroad was continually compromised, and river traffic came to a standstill. After four years of hardship, the scars of war were evident throughout Little Dixie.

When the war finally came to a close, the residents of Hannibal began to rebuild their lives. Slowly, the machines of industry began to resume business in town. R.I. Holcombe, in his voluminous 1884 book *History of Marion County, Missouri*, described the scene:

> *Our county was in a fairly prosperous condition. The country was building up and settlers were coming into the uncultivated portions. The negroes* [sic], *lately emancipated, were beginning to work and accommodate themselves to the new order of things, their former masters were accommodating* themselves *to the change, crops were bountiful, and times generally were good. Money (greenbacks) was plenty, and prices somewhat inflated. Improvements were being made everywhere…The abolition of slavery is now regarded as having been of advantage to the general prosperity of the county, as well as of the whole country, and perhaps not a dozen individuals in the county would wish to see the institution again restored. Nobody seems to have suffered by the abolition of slavery except some of the slaves themselves, whose condition now, since they have been left to shift for themselves, is infinitely worse, physically, than it was when they were held in bondage. This fact they admit, and some of them have admitted it to the writer. The large majority, however, prefer to be free, and many of them are doubtless better off with their freedom…Side by side, in peace and harmony, interested in the prosperity and perpetuity of the country alike, dwell the ex-Union soldier and the ex-Confederate. The saber has become a scythe-blade, the bayonet a pitchfork, and he is most honored now who is the best citizen, the truest patriot. Differing as to minor considerations, as is human, the one all-powerful, all-controlling sentiment is devotion to our whole country and its institutions, loyalty to this grand and glorious Union of sovereign States*—"Distinct as the billows, yet one as the sea."

Thus, by the end of the American Civil War in 1865, John and Johanna Tobin had been born into and fled subjugation and famine in Ireland, survived the harrowing voyage across the Atlantic to North America, married and become widowed, migrated west as a single parent with a young daughter in tow, settled in the Midwest, remarried and fought for the cause of the Union. Even during the midst of war, the couple showed their faith in the future by welcoming into the world their first son, Daniel, who was born on November 3, 1862. Their combined efforts revealed their belief in the ethos of the American dream: true freedom includes the opportunity for prosperity and success, and upward social mobility may be achieved through hard work. With a strong foundation of Catholic faith, the shared experience of their Irish roots and community and their continued pursuit of the ideals of freedom and prosperity, the couple joined together to make a better life for themselves and their children. As did others in their community, John and Johanna would pass on to their children the lessons they had learned throughout their lives and their beliefs in fundamental human rights and civic responsibility with the hope that the next generation of Hannibalians would have even greater opportunities to fulfill the promise of the American dream. For John and Johanna Tobin, their efforts would not be in vain.

Part II

How the Other Half Lived

Surviving *Titanic*

As *Titanic*'s survivors made their way back to New York after having been rescued by the crew of RMS *Carpathia*, Margaret sprang into action. While most sat in stunned silence, still in shock over the tragedy, many feeling the deep burning ache of grief over loved ones lost, she immediately set out to help. She was one of the lucky few who had been traveling alone aboard *Titanic*, and although she had lost good friends and many acquaintances in the disastrous sinking, her personal loss had not been as great as some. Fortunately, throughout her years of extensive overseas travel, Margaret had learned several different languages including French, Italian and German; she could now put these skills to good use when helping her fellow survivors aboard *Carpathia*, some of whom did not speak English.

Looking after the less fortunate—particularly the women, children and families from steerage—Margaret could not help but think of her beloved parents, now laid to rest at St. Mary's Cemetery in Hannibal. Some of these *Titanic* survivors had made the same choices John and Johanna Tobin had, to leave behind the place of their birth, the only home they'd ever known, in the hope of a better life in the United States. They had said goodbye to those they loved; in Ireland, families held funeral-like farewell gatherings in honor of those migrating to other countries, events that were very similar to "wakes," knowing that they would probably never meet again and grieving for them as if their loved ones had already died.

And now, after the heartbreaking experience of leaving their homeland, many of the survivors had endured further tragedy by losing their loved ones on *Titanic*. The survivors of the steerage class had, quite literally, lost everything; it was likely they had sold nearly everything they owned to pay for their journey across the Atlantic and boarded *Titanic* simply with what they could carry in a small satchel. Now, even the satchel was lost.

Margaret's heart reached out to these families, but her practical mind knew that further misfortune might lie ahead for some, particularly for the women and children who had lost their fathers, husbands, brothers or sons. It was a man's world, and their male family members were likely their sole means of support—once they reached the shore of America, immigration law mandated that if they did not have a plan to support themselves or could not prove that they had a place to live, they might simply be returned home on the next available ship, deported. Margaret simply could not sit idly by and allow this to happen.

Aboard *Carpathia*, Margaret recruited two of her fellow first-class survivors, Mrs. William Bucknell and Mrs. George Stone, and formed what would become known as the Titanic Survivors' Committee. Margaret, no stranger to fundraising, began to approach her fellow first-class survivors asking for cash, anything of value, even pledges on scraps of paper in order to raise funds that would be distributed to those in need to help them assimilate into their new world when *Carpathia* reached New York City. Madeline Astor, the young bride of John Jacob Astor IV who had boarded *Titanic* on the return voyage home after their honeymoon, immediately contributed $2,000. Margaret was touched by Madeline's generosity; to think that just a few weeks before, John, Madeline, Margaret and Helen had enjoyed such a lovely time traveling together in Egypt. Margaret was heartbroken for Madeline, being widowed so soon after being married, and was sad for the child she was carrying who would never know what a fine man John had been before his death aboard *Titanic*.

To pay tribute to the generosity of those who donated, and to surreptitiously shame those who had not yet into doing so, Margaret posted the list of contributors to the Titanic Survivors' Committee near the foot of the stairs on *Carpathia*. Miraculously, the list grew, and donations swelled to over $10,000. Her work was not yet done, though. When *Carpathia* finally arrived in the port of New York, Margaret stayed aboard, making sure that as they disembarked, those who needed

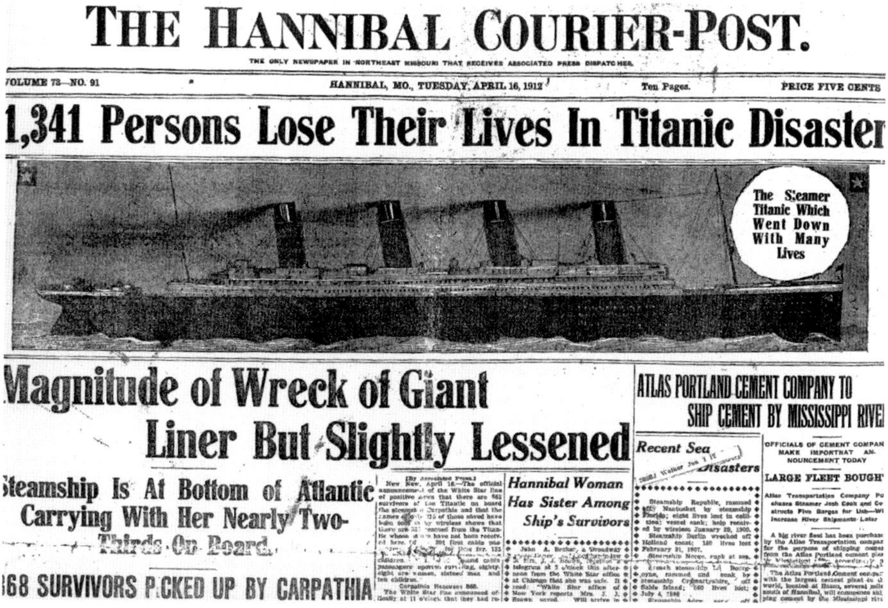

THE HANNIBAL COURIER-POST.

THE ONLY NEWSPAPER IN NORTHEAST MISSOURI THAT RECEIVES ASSOCIATED PRESS DISPATCHES.

VOLUME 73—NO. 91 HANNIBAL, MO., TUESDAY, APRIL 16, 1912 Ten Pages. PRICE FIVE CENTS

1,341 Persons Lose Their Lives In Titanic Disaster

Magnitude of Wreck of Giant Liner But Slightly Lessened

Steamship Is At Bottom of Atlantic Carrying With Her Nearly Two-Thirds On Board.

868 SURVIVORS PICKED UP BY CARPATHIA

Hannibal Woman Has Sister Among Ship's Survivors

Recent Sea Disasters

ATLAS PORTLAND CEMENT COMPANY TO SHIP CEMENT BY MISSISSIPPI RIVER

OFFICIALS OF CEMENT COMPANY MAKE IMPORTANT ANNOUNCEMENT TODAY

LARGE FLEET BOUGHT

The front page of the *Hannibal Courier-Post*, April 16, 1912. One column reported that Hannibal native Catherine Becker's sister (Margaret Tobin Brown) was listed among the survivors. *Courtesy of the* Hannibal Courier-Post.

assistance were directed to their embassies or given over to the appropriate authorities to ensure their safekeeping.

"Feeling a duty to remain after the army of Red Cross doctors and nurses, White Star officials, and general Aid Corps had taken leave of the ship," Margaret would later write, "we found it was necessary to improvise beds in the lounge, so I remained with them on board all night." When Margaret finally disembarked from the ship the next morning, she was met on the pier by her brother Daniel, who had come to New York from Hannibal, uncertain at the time of his departure as to the outcome of her fate. (The April 16, 1912 edition of the *Hannibal Courier-Post* reported that the White Star Line listed Mrs. J.J. Brown among the survivors and that her brother Daniel was en route traveling east to meet the ship, having left the afternoon before.) Daniel was relieved to see his little sister as she stepped off *Carpathia* in New York. Margaret's first concern was for the condition of her grandson; Daniel assured her that the babe was indeed fine, completely recovered, and that his illness had been brought about by sour milk. It seems as though her immediate return to the States aboard *Titanic* had not been necessary after all.

Daniel and Margaret stayed in New York City, and from their rooms at the Ritz-Carlton, they continued to aid the survivors of *Titanic*. For the next week, they would ensure that the pledges made aboard *Carpathia* were honored, the funds distributed and loved ones of the survivors contacted by telegram. As the chair of the Titanic Survivors' Committee, Margaret accepted donations on their behalf from all over the world, including $20,000 brought to them by members of the New York Stock Exchange, who had collected the funds that same day. All of the *Titanic* survivors who wished to remain in America were able to do so without fear of deportation, partly due to Margaret's efforts to provide them with the necessary means to start their new lives. Money was donated to the crew of the *Carpathia*, as well, for their heroism and generosity of spirit during the rescue. Long after the disaster, the committee would remain active, and Margaret would continue as its chairwoman throughout the remainder of her life.

Eventually, Margaret boarded a train and headed back to her home in Colorado, arriving in Denver on April 29. Margaret was one of two Denverites aboard *Titanic*; the other, Hugh R. Rood, had perished. No doubt Margaret's estranged husband, J.J. Brown, was relieved to know that Margaret had arrived safely back in Denver, but his only response upon hearing that she had survived was to say, "She's too mean to sink."

She was celebrated as the heroine of the *Titanic* disaster by newspapers across the world, but none was prouder to proclaim her as such than those in Denver. Upon her arrival, Margaret was swarmed by well-wishers and newspaper reporters clamoring to hear her firsthand account of the ordeal. Over and over again, it was requested that she relive that fateful night on the North Atlantic. *Titanic* had made her a celebrity.

On May 2, just two weeks after the sinking, Mrs. Crawford Hill held a lavish luncheon in her magnificent mansion on Sherman Street in Denver, and Margaret was to be the guest of honor. When she arrived at the luncheon, Margaret was greeted with enthusiastic applause by the privileged guests who had been invited by Mrs. Hill. This was a seminal moment in the relationship between Mrs. Hill and Mrs. Brown, and the delightful irony of this occasion would not be lost on Margaret.

Louise Sneed Hill, of the North Carolina Sneeds, was the wife of one of Denver's wealthiest businessmen, Crawford Hill, owner of the staunchly conservative newspaper *Denver Republican*. Mrs. Hill, who believed herself to be the "arbiter of Denver society," was famous for having identified Denver's Sacred Thirty-Six, a posh group of socialites whom she declared to be the only members of Denver's elite worthy of an invitation to her extravagant parties. J.J. and Margaret Brown—because of their Irish roots, Catholic faith and "new money"—were not on Mrs. Hill's list, nor were many other notable wealthy Denverites.

Margaret, however, was by no means a social outcast in Denver simply because she was not a member of the Sacred Thirty-Six; to the contrary, Margaret was invited to many of the same parties as Mrs. Crawford Hill, and both worked together as members of charitable and social committees in Denver for years. No doubt their differences in politics and attitudes toward those less fortunate kept Mrs. Hill and Mrs. Brown from being close friends, but they certainly regarded each other as friendly acquaintances.

However, for Mrs. Crawford Hill to not only invite Margaret to her home but also make her the guest of honor must have been quite a moment for Margaret. She graciously attended the luncheon, then returned the favor by hosting an event of her own for Mrs. Hill in the House of Lions a short time later. If these events had occurred when Margaret had first arrived in Denver in 1895, she would have been delighted to be accepted by Denver society; now, nearly twenty years later, Margaret had leapfrogged over those in Denver society and was simply amused by the idea that Mrs. Hill had finally acquiesced. Margaret could see through the veneer and knew that Mrs. Hill simply couldn't resist being a part of Margaret's newfound fame after *Titanic*.

As far as Margaret was concerned, one of the triumphs of her life was to overcome the challenges of her childhood poverty as the daughter of "Famine Irish" Catholics. To be celebrated in the society columns of newspapers around the world was comeuppance for all those times over the years that others had tried to hold her back, to use her poor upbringing in Hannibal against her. Margaret never apologized for her family or her background; it was who she was, and if someone didn't care for it, it was no concern of hers. But there was no question that Margaret did all that she could to overcome the limitations of her social status at birth. She would spend her life improving her situation and her station in life.

Overachieving above what others believed you should be able to accomplish was a trait she had certainly learned during her childhood in Hannibal.

Molly Brown's Hannibal

The postwar years of Reconstruction brought about great change and unbridled ambition to the citizens of Hannibal. Shaking off the shackles of war, both literally and figuratively, Hannibalians seized their chance at a "new birth of freedom" and set out to bring unprecedented prosperity and wealth to the booming river town. The Hannibal & St. Joseph Railroad had not only survived the war but also gained nationwide attention as an important railway, the main rail line to the emerging markets of the Wild West, an opportunity that businessmen in Hannibal were eager to exploit. The industry that would emerge as the strongest and most valuable during this time was lumbering.

Although the lumber industry began along the Mississippi River in the 1830s, it wasn't until after the Civil War that sawmills dominated the Hannibal riverfront. Enterprising lumbermen from around the country set up shop in Hannibal, buying from the seemingly inexhaustible supply of white pine logs from Wisconsin and Minnesota, tying the logs into rafts, floating the rafts down the Mississippi and milling the logs into lumber along the Hannibal levee and the banks of Bear Creek. After it was milled, the finished lumber could then be sent to markets south by steamboat or west by train. Beginning in the late 1860s and continuing throughout the 1880s, as the South was being rebuilt after the war and the West was being "won," the demand for lumber was immense, and Hannibal would become the fourth-largest lumber center in the United States. The entrepreneurs who had the foresight to set up the lumber firms in Hannibal became absolute millionaires. At its peak, sixteen privately owned Hannibal lumberyards were producing a combined total of more than 230 million linear feet of lumber per year.

Not only did the lumber firms have their headquarters in Hannibal, but most of the owners lived in town, as well. Thus, as their wealth increased, the money stayed in the local economy, and the entire town prospered. These lumber barons, as they came to be called, became the leaders in the community and were responsible for putting into place the infrastructure of the town: building bridges and railroads, financing civic improvements such as parks and churches, opening banks and financing lumber-related businesses such as woodworking shops that produced moldings, sashes, doors, corbels, stairs and newel posts.

Throughout the era of the lumber barons, Hannibal would continually overachieve, successfully competing with cities ten times its size. It was the "little city that could," a town that would set an incredibly high goal and then somehow rally together to realize the dream. For example, before the Civil War, prosperous lumber mills could be found in Quincy, Illinois (twenty miles northeast of Hannibal); Louisiana, Missouri (another Mississippi River town about thirty miles south of Hannibal); and St. Louis, Missouri. By 1870, those firms had closed up shop, some actually relocating to Hannibal. With each triumph, the enthusiasm of the town's residents increased, and their dreams for the future grew. As Hannibal's population reached about twelve thousand souls and the annual business revenue topped out at around $15 million per year, the publishers of the Hannibal City Directory of 1871, Charles Banzhaf and John L. Ransom, encouraged new businesses to locate in Hannibal by optimistically declaring:

> *There is good room, without trenching much upon the hills, for* two thousand first class business houses—*none farther than half a mile from the river or from railroad depot. Two thousand such establishments, occupied by enterprising, pushing men, with suitable capital, would easily accommodate an annual business of* two hundred million dollars—*or, if necessary, double that amount. Such facts show our possibilities, and that we have substantial grounds upon which to build and maintain a city of half a million population.*

As Hannibal ushered in this new era of prosperity, John and Johanna Tobin welcomed their second child together: a daughter, Margaret, whom they called Maggie. The babe was born on Thursday, July 18, 1867, in the small bedroom of the Tobin home on Denkler's Alley. Little Maggie was an instant favorite of her older half-sister, Katie, now ten years old, and the two would become inseparable. The Tobin family would grow larger with the births of William in 1869 and Helen in 1871, bringing the total number of John and Johanna's children to six.

Although the Irish who resided in the area around Denkler's Alley would work long, laborious hours for very little income and would have been considered among the poorest residents in Hannibal at that time, they did their best to live happily. John Tobin's modest home featured a summer kitchen on the lower level that was adjacent to the indoor stall where the family's milk cow and chickens were kept. Due to the severe slope of the hill against which the house was built, the south side of the building where the front door and sitting room were situated was actually at ground level, but to the north, where the bedroom was located over the summer kitchen,

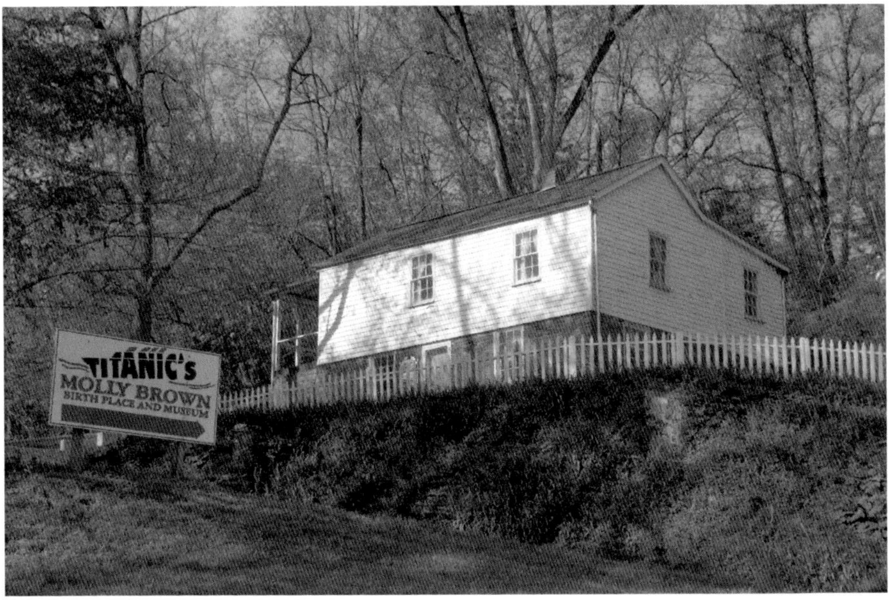

Margaret Tobin Brown's birthplace on Denkler's Alley. The house has been fully restored on its original site and is now a museum in Hannibal. *Courtesy of Hannibal Convention and Visitors Bureau.*

it had the appearance of a two-story structure. This dwelling was similar in style and size to others in the neighborhood and, though small and sparsely furnished, was able to adequately accommodate the family's needs.

By all accounts, the Tobin siblings enjoyed a very happy upbringing. The neighborhood children, mostly Irish, some of whom were Tobin cousins, would have had innumerable opportunities to keep themselves entertained in and around Hannibal. On warm summer days, Maggie and her cohorts would have spent time searching for frogs and other wildlife along the shores of the Mississippi River just a few blocks away from their home. Or, upon hearing the carnival-like tunes that emanated from steam-powered calliopes echoing off the bluffs along the river, they would have climbed nearby Cardiff Hill to have a bird's-eye view of the massive steamboats as they came ashore along Hannibal's levee. There would be swimming in Bear Creek, trips to McDaniel's Confectionery on Main Street for colorful candies and delicious roasted nuts, and lively community celebrations in Central Park. When they dared, Maggie and her friends might have sometimes ventured just south of Lover's Leap, clutching fire-laden torches, and carefully creeped into the moist, hollow blackness of the spooky labyrinth of limestone caves, just as

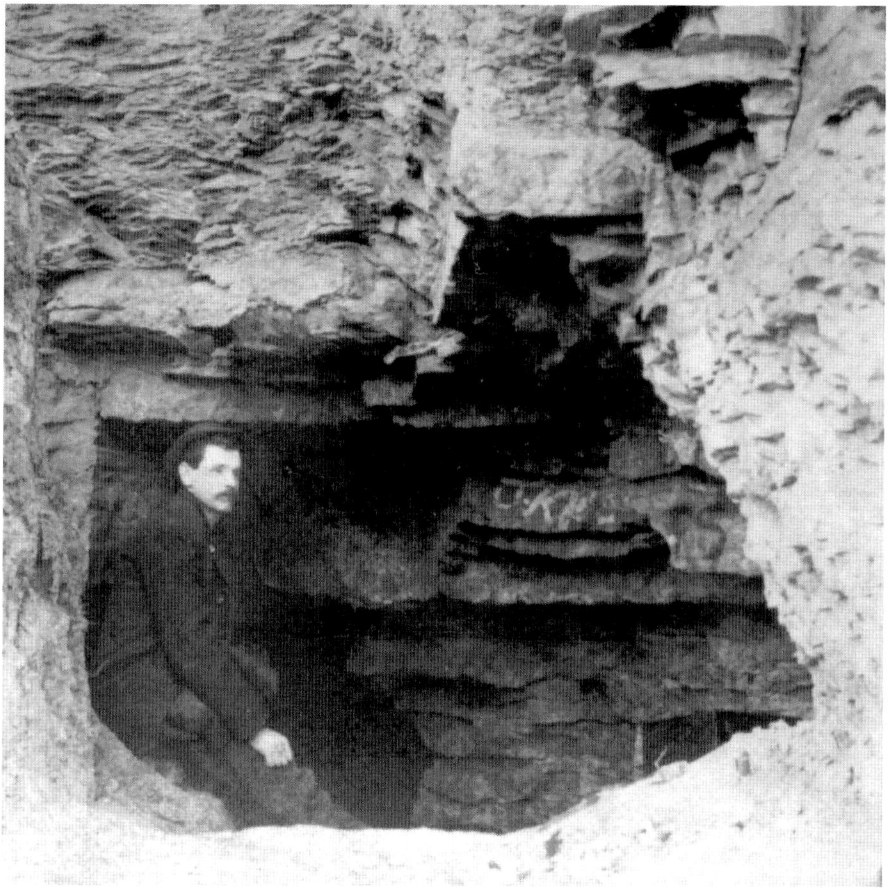

Nineteenth-century entrance to the caves in Hannibal made famous by Mark Twain in *The Adventures of Tom Sawyer*. *Courtesy of Steve Chou.*

Samuel Clemens had done as a boy some thirty years earlier. In winter, when heavy snows draped the city in blankets of white, the slope of Denkler's Alley would come alive with the squeals and laughter of both children and adults alike as they enjoyed tobogganing down the steep, slippery hill.

Education would also be a very important component of Maggie's childhood. In his unpublished manuscript entitled "Memories of a Grandson," Margaret Brown's grandson, James Benziger, wrote, "Grandmother [Johanna] Tobin was a skimmer…She would look over the front page of a newspaper, complain of her glasses, and then ask whatever young person was at hand to read certain stories. All the young people were convinced that she had never learned to read easily." It is probable that Johanna was illiterate, particularly after having been born into an Ireland where Catholics were given little to no opportunity to attend school. It was therefore extremely important to Johanna that her children receive a good education.

Before the Civil War, most Hannibalians believed that education was the responsibility of the family and that public education was for the poorer classes that needed charity, unable to afford to educate their children privately. As a result, for many years, there was general opposition to government-sponsored education, believing that it was unfair for every family to pay a tax for education regardless of whether or not their family had children of school age. After the war, the education of the freed slaves became an issue across the country, and the idea of free public schools for all children, regardless of race or socioeconomic background, began to take shape. In 1866, the Hannibal School District was organized, charging tuition to those who could afford it, and for those who were unable, the city would cover their fees through a tax levy. Eighty-nine students were enrolled the first year; by 1870, more than one thousand Hannibal children were attending school, including "colored" children, whose school was separate but still funded by city government (in 1868, the Missouri legislature passed a state law requiring that separate schools for "Negroes" were mandatory).

From the 1871 Hannibal City Directory:

> *This school is the nursery of talented and industrious students, and open to the poor as freely as the rich. Thus the path to learning and ambition is open to all, and by this provision it is anticipated that the city will secure for herself and the country the cultivated talents of her gifted children. The free schools are supported by a special tax, known as the school tax, collected as other revenues, by the Collector of the county, and varies in amount from 1 to 1⅓ per cent tax upon the taxable property of the city…In a few years it is hoped that public sentiment will finally settle upon the free school system as the best and only means of securing that universal popular education, which lies at the basis of popular liberty. Free schools and a free government are inseparable.*

All of the Tobin children, including Maggie, attended Mrs. O'Leary's grammar school on Prospect Avenue just a few blocks from their home. Although Mary O'Leary was Maggie's aunt, many of the neighborhood children were also her pupils. Not only is it likely that Mrs. O'Leary's school was the one nearest to Denkler's Alley, but it is also probable that rather than attend the new public school as a "charity case," the Tobins preferred to send their children to a "private" school as an outward showing of their financial independence and an attempt to overcome the perception of their lower income status.

For as Hannibal became a center of industry, the chasm between the socioeconomic classes would become even wider. The rich would become richer, and while many of the poor would struggle to rise out of poverty, only a few would have the opportunity to climb the ladder of success. Although John Tobin was known to be a hard worker and was able to adequately provide for his family, most likely his lack of formal education relegated him to work as a low-paid laborer at the gasworks, where he remained throughout Maggie's childhood.

The Gilded Age of Hannibal

America emerged from the difficult years of Reconstruction and, by 1877, had awoken to the dawn of a new era known as the Gilded Age. The term first appeared as the name of a book written by none other than Hannibal's own Mark Twain, co-written with Charles Dudley Warner in 1873. *The Gilded Age: A Tale of Today* was a satirical look at social issues of the time being glossed over by the rich with the "veneer of a layer of gold." The Gilded Age in the United States was a time of enormous growth: populations increased with the influx of immigrants clamoring to become Americans; technological advances that made transportation, manufacturing and communication more efficient were creating new industries and providing jobs at all skill levels; and an emerging middle class worked hard and spent money on newfangled, machine-made clothing, entertainment and home furnishings.

Hannibal was no exception. Because Hannibal was a central hub of railroad activity, culture and sophistication came to Hannibal more so than in other towns of similar size; comparatively, Hannibal was a very cosmopolitan town, with access to goods and services that rivaled the much larger midwestern urban centers of St. Louis and Chicago. As the wealthy in Hannibal began to build impressive Victorian mansions and participate in glamorous social events, they would require the finest in furniture, foodstuffs, clothing and carriages. Merchants were happy to oblige.

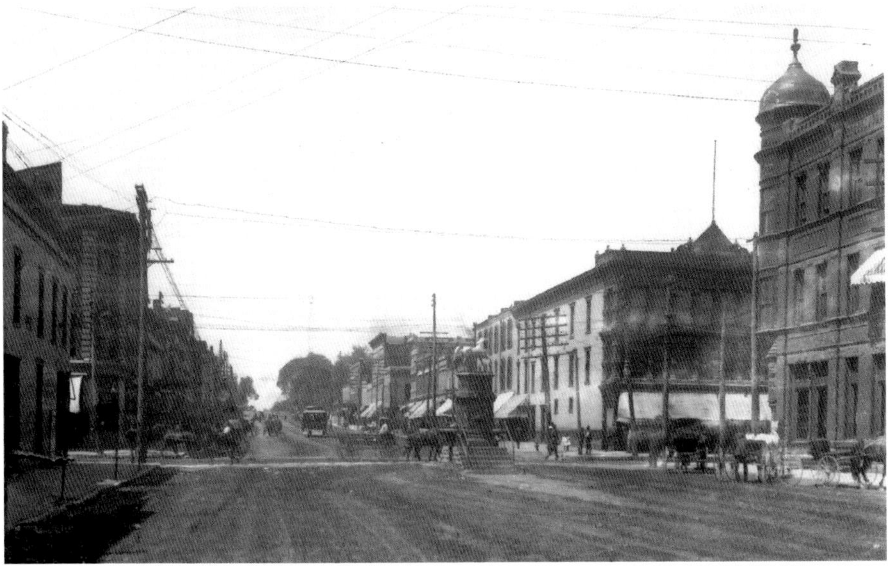

In this view of Broadway, looking west from Main Street, one can note both the drinking fountain (for man and horse) and an early streetcar in the distance. *Courtesy of Steve Chou.*

All along Main Street and Broadway, ladies' dress shops began to appear, displaying in their windows the latest fashions from Paris, silk gowns with padded hips, bustles and long trains profusely trimmed with pleated ruffles and beading that replaced the outdated look of hoop skirts. Millinery shops displayed elaborate chapeaux for the ladies with exotic bird feathers alongside fine beaver-skinned top hats for the gentlemen. Accessories such as lace parasols, pleated fans, hair adornments and fancy kid leather gloves became necessary. Shoe stores, too, could be found in this new fashion district, the shoes being custom made to fit at the hands of German cobblers in workrooms housed on the second floors above the stores.

As a young girl, Maggie Tobin could have stepped out the front door of her home, climbed less than one block up the bluff where Denkler's Alley turns into Sixth Street, turned left onto North Street and walked one block over to Fifth Street in order to view the spectacle of Millionaires' Row. Nicknamed in the 1870s and still referred to as such today, Fifth Street was the address wealthy Hannibalians wanted. As Maggie would walk south along Millionaires' Row, she would have borne witness to block after block of newly constructed, magnificent Victorian homes: Judge Joseph Rowe's three-story French-inspired Second Empire home on the southeast corner of Fifth and North that featured a copula for viewing the river, completed in 1870;

the Queen Anne–style Pettibone Mansion one block down at 313 North Fifth Street, with its round turrets and wraparound porch, first built in 1871 and enlarged several times over the next twenty years; lumber baron David Dubach's splendid home on the southwest corner of Fifth and Bird Streets, a three-story amalgamation of an Italianate Villa, Queen Anne and Second Empire rolled into one, also completed in 1871; Fred Dubach's enormous Italianate located diagonally across from his brother's home on the northeast corner of Fifth and Bird, with its lacy, wrought-iron accoutrements around

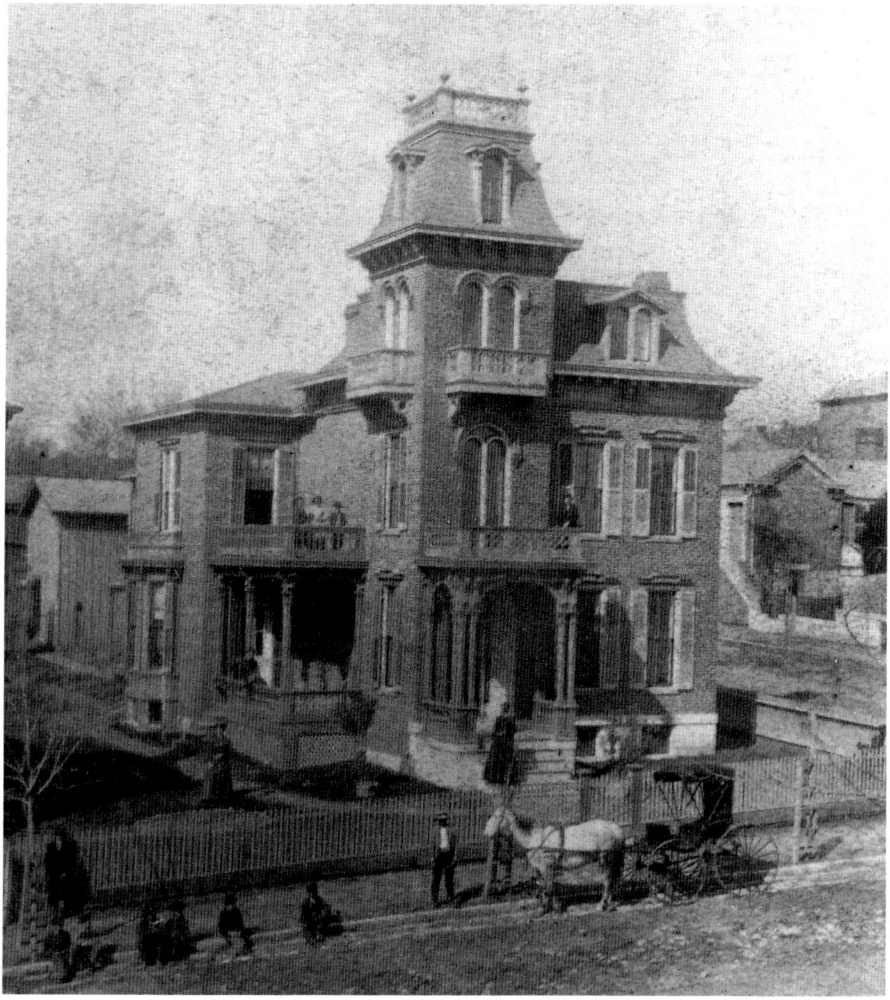

Lumber baron David Dubach's home on Millionaires' Row (Fifth Street) on the southwest corner at Bird Street, built in 1871. Today, this is the Dubach Inn Bed-and-Breakfast owned by Steve and Kristine Russell. *Courtesy of Steve Chou.*

the roofline, built in 1866; and dozens of other amazing homes that stretched down the eight blocks of Millionaires' Row from North Street to the edge of the bluff just south of Lyon, where Fifth Street terminated. The houses along Millionaires' Row—these grand structures with their elaborate corbels, deep gables, multilayered wood trims, wraparound porches with fancy turned wood spindles, balconies providing rooms with a view and grand oak front doors with leaded glass windows—would have seemed massive compared to the three-room cottage to which Maggie and her family would have been accustomed.

Other structures were going up in Hannibal at this time, but none was more eagerly anticipated or more important to the town's future than the first bridge in Hannibal to allow easy crossing of the Mississippi River between the shores of Illinois and Missouri. The bridge would usurp the need for ferry service across the river and make access available in the winter months regardless of whether the river froze over. It would also allow the Hannibal & St. Joseph Railroad and other railway lines to be directly connected to trains from the East for the first time.

In 1869, the Hannibal Bridge Company was incorporated to design and construct the new bridge at a cost of $485,000. The site selected for the bridge marked the narrowest point of the river south of Galena, Illinois, some 1,300 feet wide. Unfortunately, to accommodate this location, the bridge would reach Missouri and abruptly face the side of a massive bluff; therefore, a 302-foot tunnel had to be blasted through the limestone for the rail line to continue on its path. For months, the residents of Hannibal endured thunderous booms ricocheting off the side of the bluffs along the river as nitroglycerin charges were detonated, shaking the very foundation of the town and rattling the nerves of those who lived closest to the area. Unfortunately for the Tobin family, the bluff being blasted was very near Denkler's Alley just to the north of Cardiff Hill.

The new bridge featured both rail lines and wooden planks so that pedestrians and wagon teams might also cross. The original toll rates for use of the bridge were: footman, five cents; man and horse, fifteen cents; man, vehicle and one horse, twenty cents; man, vehicle and two horses, thirty cents; hogs, sheep or goats, three cents each; and horses, cattle or mules, six cents each.

Always eager to have a reason to celebrate, the citizens of Hannibal turned out en masse for the Hannibal Bridge's grand opening held on August 1, 1871 (also referred to as the Wabash Bridge in honor of the railway that helped finance its construction). Crowds gathered along the river's edge to watch

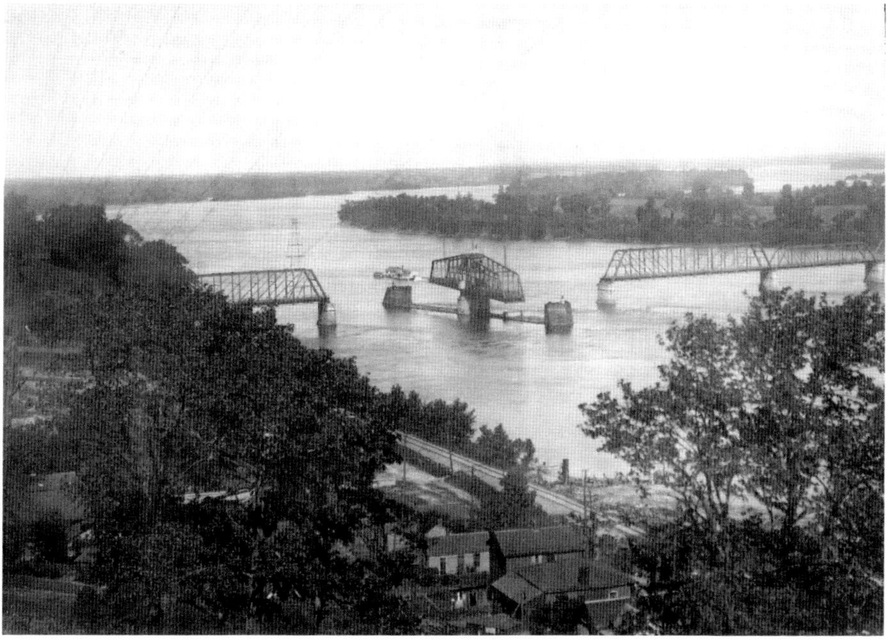

Hannibal's Wabash Bridge, completed in 1871, provided one of the few routes for a train to cross the upper Mississippi at the time. *Courtesy of Steve Chou.*

the swinging steel span near the Missouri shore revolve horizontally, allowing steamboats to pass unimpeded. Some, perhaps even members of the Tobin family, climbed to the top of the newly christened Tunnel Hill (one of the bluffs located today in Riverview Park) to have the vantage point directly over the tunnel; here they could have witnessed the thrilling sight of the first train crossing the bridge, driven slowly and with great apprehension by the aptly named engineer, W.C. Bridges of Hannibal, and watched as the mighty locomotive disappeared into the tunnel beneath their feet.

Panic Facilitates Philanthropy

The Hannibal Bridge was just one of the thousands of advancements made by American railroad companies after the Civil War. More than thirty-three thousand miles of new track had been laid between 1868 and 1873, zigzagging across the United States and financed with the help of government land grants and subsidies to the railroads. Second only to agriculture as the nation's largest employer, the railroad industry generated massive cash infusions from speculators who wanted to cash in on the boom; this unfortunately caused abnormally rapid growth in the rail companies, as well as the overbuilding of factories and ancillary facilities, high-risk investments that offered no immediate or guaranteed returns.

These rampant speculative investments in the railroad industry—when added to postwar inflation, a large trade deficit and significant property losses suffered with the devastating Chicago Fire of 1871 and Boston Fire of 1872—strained the nation's capital reserves to the brink of collapse. When the Federal Reserve in New York City plummeted from $50 million to just $17 million in September and October 1873, the country plunged into economic recession. The Panic of 1873 was a major financial setback across the United States and deeply affected the lives of the citizenry of Hannibal.

As Hannibal businesses felt the effects of the recession, cuts in production and expenses were made. Unemployment began to rise, particularly for those unskilled laborers at the railroad yards, lumber mills and large manufacturing plants. Merchants saw their sales decrease; those who had money began to hold on to it, resisting the urge to spend as freely as they had previously.

In the years before federal income tax, the poor and indigent relied on the charity of their community to help them through times such as these. During the Panic of 1873, which did not abate in Hannibal until late in 1874, no unemployment insurance or welfare was available from the federal government, nor were there any state agencies to apply to for relief or that would provide aid in securing employment. The civic leaders in Hannibal began to have great concerns as to how to manage the financial crisis as more of their fellow citizens were going hungry and losing their homes.

A coalition of businessmen stepped up and agreed to support a place that would provide temporary shelter for those in need. The members leased a tenement house near the Denkler's Alley neighborhood, just across from the Hannibal gasworks at Fourth Street and Palmyra Avenue. The building was owned by William Walden, who was paid $35.00 per month for its use. $300.00 was also spent to furnish the space, which would allow thirty residents to find accommodations. Townsfolk took to calling the facility "City Hospital," long before a bona fide hospital would be built in Hannibal. Mrs. Louis Webb was hired at $50.00 per month to take charge of the facility, and the doors were officially opened in December 1873. In 1874, a total of $6,013.35 was reported to have been spent on the welfare of those in need.

This demonstrates that although the class structure of the Victorian era was emblematic in Hannibal, the town's wealthy were also very philanthropic and were always eager to contribute to the common good. Hannibalians were a people prone to organize; each time a new idea was brought forth, a committee would be formed to manage the effort. Numerous civic organizations were incorporated, with many of the same prominent businessmen called to lead multiple boards. These leaders in the community frequently came together and unselfishly financed and supervised efforts to overcome some of the most important issues facing the town to the betterment of all Hannibalians.

However, it was not only the wealthy who would contribute to the common good. Benevolent societies and fraternal organizations could be found in Hannibal as early as the 1840s, and while some catered to the rich, many of these organizations welcomed to their membership those of modest financial means. Groups such as Chapter Number 7 of the Royal Arch Masons, the Excalibur Commandery Number 5 Knights Templar, Mystic Lodge No. 17 of the International Order of Odd Fellows and the Irish Benevolent Society were formed in Hannibal not only to foster camaraderie but also out of a genuine desire to provide assistance to their members and the community at large, fulfilling the need for services not yet considered a function of state or federal government. Through volunteerism and fundraising, these groups would have an increasingly important effect on improving the quality of life for all Hannibalians.

Although most of the fraternal and benevolent groups were segregated by race and gender, women would not be left out. Forming auxiliary lodges, benevolent societies and independent woman's clubs of their own, their activities were related particularly to education, social reform and the care of Hannibal's neediest children. Because women were excluded from many positions of power and influence in society during the Victorian era, some women undoubtedly used these clubs as outlets for their energies and discovered their talent for organization and management. Groups would gather to sew clothing to donate to various relief organizations managed by local churches or host charitable fundraising events to raise money for innumerable causes. Often, the best way for women to help further their causes was to convince their husbands to support the causes as well.

As each of the Tobin children reached the age of thirteen, and after graduating from Mrs. O'Leary's grammar school, they were expected to find work to help ease the family's burdens. Maggie's elder sister, Katie, was the first to leave the nest, taking a position in 1873 as a live-in servant at the home of S.W. Leslie at 205 South Eighth Street. In addition to the fine homes on Millionaires' Row, many other homes of large stature could be found on Fourth, Sixth, Seventh and Eighth Streets, as well as on the cross-streets of Bird, Center, Broadway, Church and Lyon. Many of

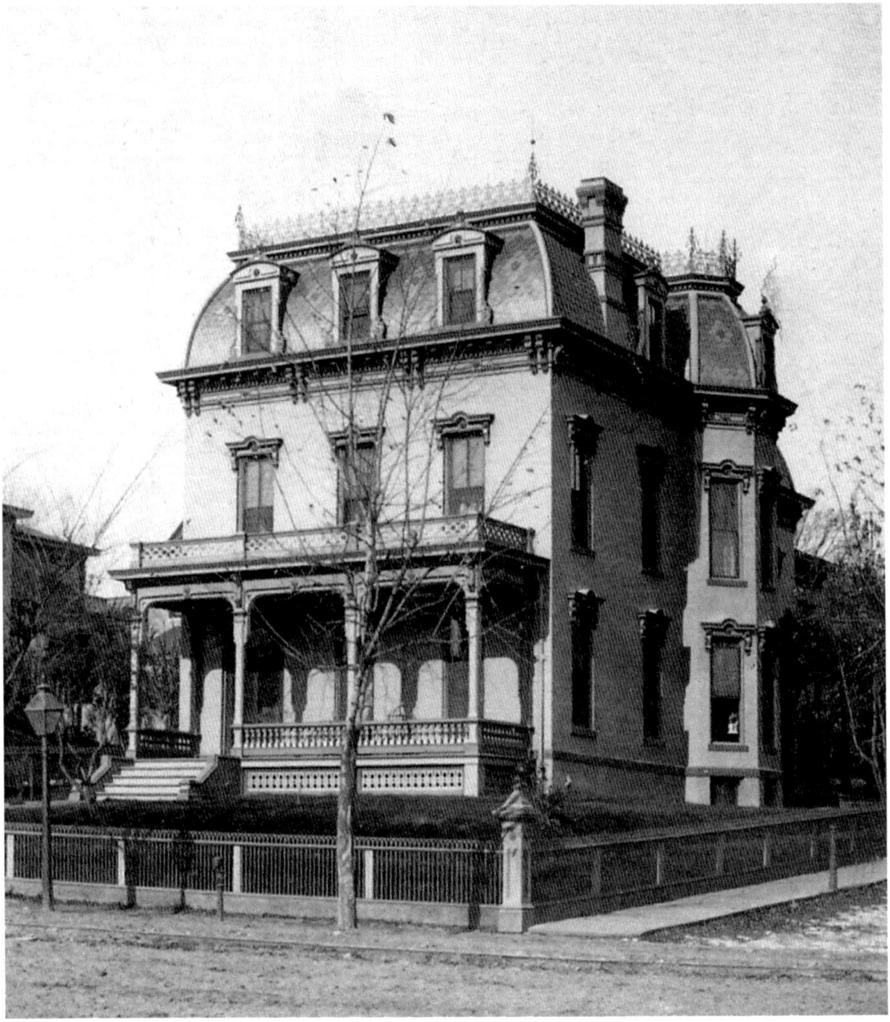

The David Dulany home on Broadway, one of the elegant Victorian homes built during Margaret Tobin's childhood. *Courtesy of Steve Chou.*

these homes were equipped with servant's quarters and employed young Irish ladies as domestics for cleaning, cooking and other household duties. Often, neighbors shared servants for special occasions when additional help was required. While Katie performed her domestic duties, she may have provided her younger sister with the opportunity to catch a rare glimpse at the interiors of these fine homes.

One can imagine the dreams this would have inspired, the idea of living in one of these impressive mansions—lavish dinners served on gleaming silver trays by white-gloved domestics, the comfort of an enormous feather bed that you didn't have to share with siblings, plush carpets soft under one's feet stretched across perfectly polished hardwood floors, marble-topped tables displaying whatnots collected on trips abroad to exotic locations and the soft glow of gaslights illuminating walls covered with Lincrusta papers imported from Europe that featured hand-rubbed twenty-four-carat gold dust on their textured surfaces. To see firsthand how the "other half" lived would have certainly left an indelible impression on the young Irish lass living on Denkler's Alley.

Part III

Women in a Man's World

After the tragedy aboard *Titanic*, Margaret decided to take a house in Newport, Rhode Island; she had long before outgrown Denver and was eager to start a new chapter in her life. In August 1909, J.J. and Margaret had agreed to a legal separation, which allowed Margaret to keep their Denver home, the House of Lions on Pennsylvania Avenue, and provided her with a trust fund of $25,000 (less than 10 percent of J.J.'s net worth at the time). Margaret believed she could live comfortably from fees collected from tenants renting the House of Lions and from the monthly interest generated by the trust fund.

The decision to legally separate had been a difficult one for Margaret. Although there were rumors of unfaithfulness on his part, this was only one of the many issues the marriage faced. J.J. could not abide by Margaret's Progressive Era ideals; he was very much a man used to Victorian social norms and was known to say, "A woman's name should appear in the newspaper only four times in her life: at her birth, engagement, marriage, and death." He was a mining industrialist; she continually fought for miners' rights, eight-hour workdays and safer working conditions. He was socially conservative; she thrived with friends considered *avant-garde*. He loved the rugged terrain of the West; she longed for the fineries of the salons in New York. He grew tired of overseas travel; she adored Paris, in particular, and was always eager to explore new lands. The more he tried to keep her grounded, the more she seemed to want to fly. Their disagreements became bitter, but divorce for a Catholic couple was simply not an option.

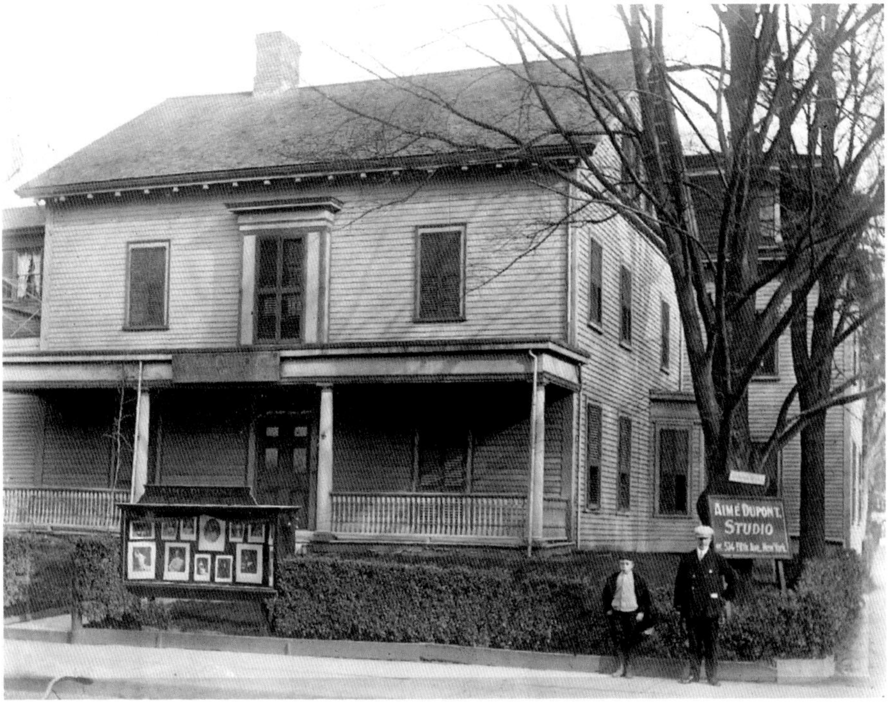

Margaret named her twenty-three-room cottage in Newport Mon Etui. This house was turned into an American Red Cross hospital and rehabilitation center during World War I. *Courtesy of the Newport Historical Society.*

Moving away from her life with J.J., Margaret formed new alliances with like-minded contemporaries who summered in the stunning mansions of Rhode Island's famous coastal community. Margaret had been a frequent guest at Newport since 1909, visiting her friends John Astor, Alva Vanderbilt Belmont and the Contessa Leary, but now, in the summer following her experience aboard *Titanic*, she decided to settle there, leasing a large but (compared to her friends) "modest" twenty-three-room cottage at 44 Bellevue Avenue that she named Mon Etui.

Beginning in 1852 with the construction of Chateau-sur-Mer, the home of William Shepard Wetmore, Newport had become a summer resort for wealthy East Coast families. With the completion of William Vanderbilt's remarkable fifty-room Marble House, completed in 1892, Newport earned a reputation as the summer playground of the wealthiest and most elite of the New York social scene. Marble House, modeled after the Petit Trianon at Versailles, cost an estimated $11 million at the time and featured 500,000 cubic feet of imported white marble.

Not to be outdone, William's elder brother, Cornelius Vanderbilt II, commissioned the construction of his sixty-five-thousand-square-foot Newport mansion, The Breakers, completed in 1895. Always concerned about fire, Vanderbilt insisted the home be built without the use of timbers; instead, the fireproof building was built with steel trusses surrounded by Indiana limestone. The five-story, seventy-room Italian Renaissance castle was the largest and most costly of the Newport homes, estimated at $13 million. Other magnificent homes for the wealthy soon followed, and by the turn of the century, Newport was world-renowned as the epitome of American life during the Gilded Age, immortalized in popular novels of the time by Edith Wharton and Henry James.

Although Newport society included some of the wealthiest people in the world, Mrs. J.J. Brown was a welcomed member. Many of the women of Newport were social activists, several of whom, such as Alva Vanderbilt Belmont, participated in the women's suffrage movement, of which Margaret had been keenly involved for the past twenty years. Women in these circles had more individual freedoms than most of their generation—they were expected to be well educated, free to travel with or without their husbands and took a particular interest in politics, all issues that most Americans in the Victorian era believed were taboo for ladies of refinement. The women of Newport, because of their wealth, held positions of influence and power and used their positions to affect great change. Margaret fit in with them perfectly.

On August 14, 1912, Madeline Astor gave birth to a son, John Jacob Astor VI (a cousin, John Jacob Astor V, was born before Madeline's son). To welcome the birth of the baby, and as a way to honor the victims of *Titanic*, Margaret hosted an event at Mon Etui to raise funds toward a new maternity ward at the hospital in Newport. The program she selected, "Songs of Old France," was performed entirely in French. It was reported that one hundred of the Newport ladies who attended the fundraiser pledged their support in financing the new ward.

Seemingly undaunted by her *Titanic* experience, Margaret was once again aboard an ocean liner just six months later in the fall of 1912. Princess Stephanie Dolgoruky had invited her to spend the winter in Russia, and after an extended stay in St. Petersburg, Margaret made her way once again to Bombay, toured India and then met her daughter Helen in Paris in the early spring of 1913.

Helen had, just two months before, announced her engagement to George Benziger, thirteen years her senior. George's family owned Benziger Brothers Publishing and was responsible for publishing all of the Roman

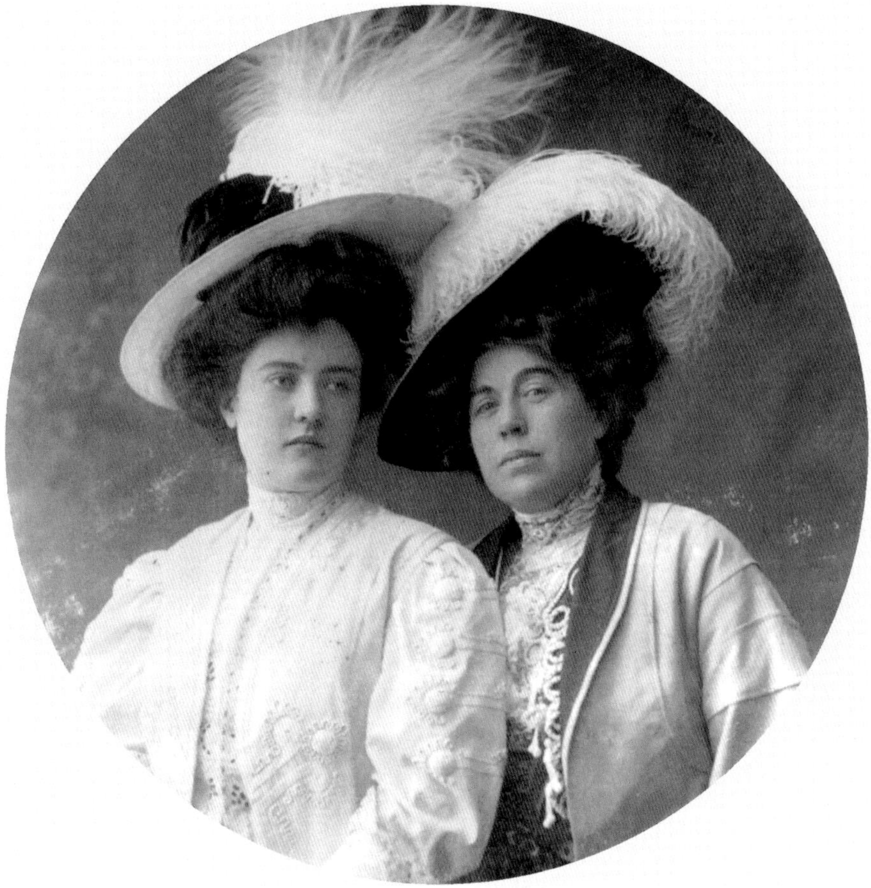

Margaret posing with daughter Helen. *Courtesy of History Colorado, 10025892.*

Catholic catechisms, as well as priests' concordances to the Bible. George's mother was of the Von Saarentein family, the daughter of a Swiss count and countess, and two of his sisters were married to Austrian barons.

Although Margaret liked George and approved of the marriage, she did not return to the United States for Helen's wedding. She chose instead to travel through Germany. This may have been, in part, to avoid an encounter with J.J.; Margaret knew that he would be on hand to give the bride away, as Helen always had a very close relationship with her father. Margaret believed that Helen would understand her mother's decision not to attend the wedding—surely Helen would know that Margaret was with her in spirit if not in person.

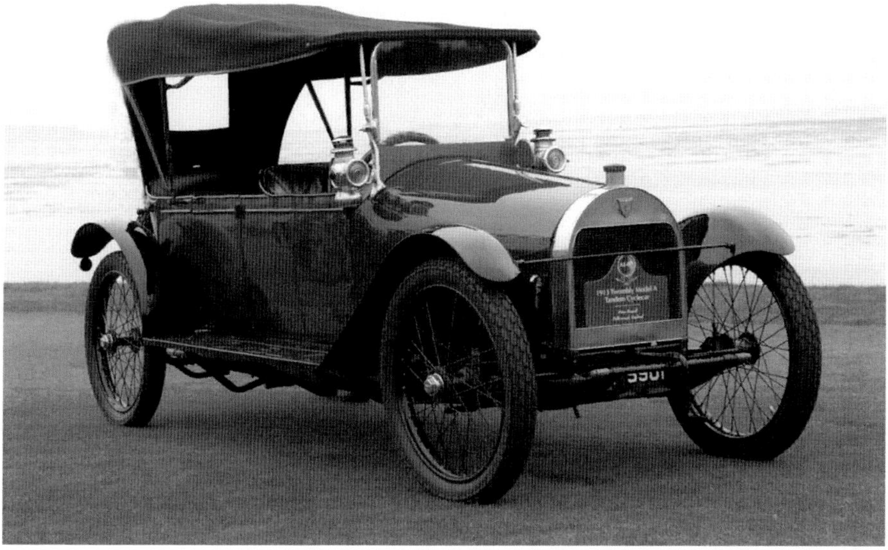

The Twombly Cycle car, built between 1913 and 1915. This is the first automobile purchased by Margaret for her home in Newport, Rhode Island. *Author's collection.*

Upon her return to Newport for the 1913 social season, Margaret took the town by storm. "[Mrs. Brown] thundered into Newport," reported one of the newspapers. "This season she is entertaining society in a lavish manner. (I mean she entertains them at home, and not only by the things she says.) Newport is entirely conscious that she is present, and they say she is the best-dressed woman in the place."

Margaret had gained a reputation as one of the most fashionable ladies everywhere she went, spending heavily on her trips to Paris and bringing home with her the most up-to-date styles. She also caused quite a stir when she purchased her first automobile for guests to drive when they visited Newport, a Twombly Cycle car. This sporty little convertible featured one front seat and one back seat—meaning room for one person in the front, the driver, and one person in the back, a passenger. Naturally, Margaret learned to drive the car herself. That year, 1913, Margaret was described by the *Newport Herald* as being one of the most unique residents of Newport; her home had become a place "for people of taste and accomplishment."

Champions for the Rights of Women, Children and Workers

Alva Vanderbilt Belmont had a lot in common with Margaret Tobin Brown. Although not born into poverty, Alva was the daughter of Murray and Phoebe Smith of Mobile, Alabama, a rural yet bustling town in the mid-eighteenth century. After being tutored at a private girls' boarding school in France, Alva was acutely aware of the path her life was to take—devoted wife and mother—and dreaded it. "There was a static quality to a girl's life, a monotony and restriction in it from which I rebelled from the very first," she was quoted as saying. "My first experiences in life gave birth to my belief in militant woman suffrage."

She dutifully married but did quite well for herself, pursuing and landing William Kissam Vanderbilt, arguably the most eligible bachelor in the United States. She married at the age of twenty-two in 1875, and she instantly became a leader in New York's social circles. When Willie's father died, leaving him a $70 million inheritance, the Vanderbilts began to design a magnificent palace in Newport, Rhode Island, to entertain their summer guests. Marble House was completed in 1888, and despite the outward appearances the couple tried to maintain, there was trouble with the marriage. Willie was a philanderer; although infidelity was not uncommon at the time, and most women were relegated to tolerating it as long as a certain degree of discretion could be maintained, Alva was not the typical wife willing to "look the other way." To the shock and disapproval of many, Alva filed for divorce from William in 1894.

Alva was able to retain Marble House, as William had given her full ownership as a gift for her thirty-ninth birthday the year before. She was granted custody of their three children, alimony of $100,000 per year and the right to keep the Vanderbilt name. Although initially ostracized by her society friends, some came to realize that they, too, were not willing to tolerate similar behavior in their husbands and filed for divorces as well. Although Margaret would not divorce J.J., one of the contributing factors to their separation had been rumors of infidelity, and to Margaret's horror, some of the rumors had even been reported in the society columns of newspapers back west.

Two years later, Alva married Oliver Hazard Perry Belmont. Oliver, son of the wealthy financier August Belmont, also owned a magnificent home in Newport: Belcourt Castle, a fifty-thousand-square-foot French Renaissance structure modeled after Louis XIII's hunting lodge at Versailles. Oliver was

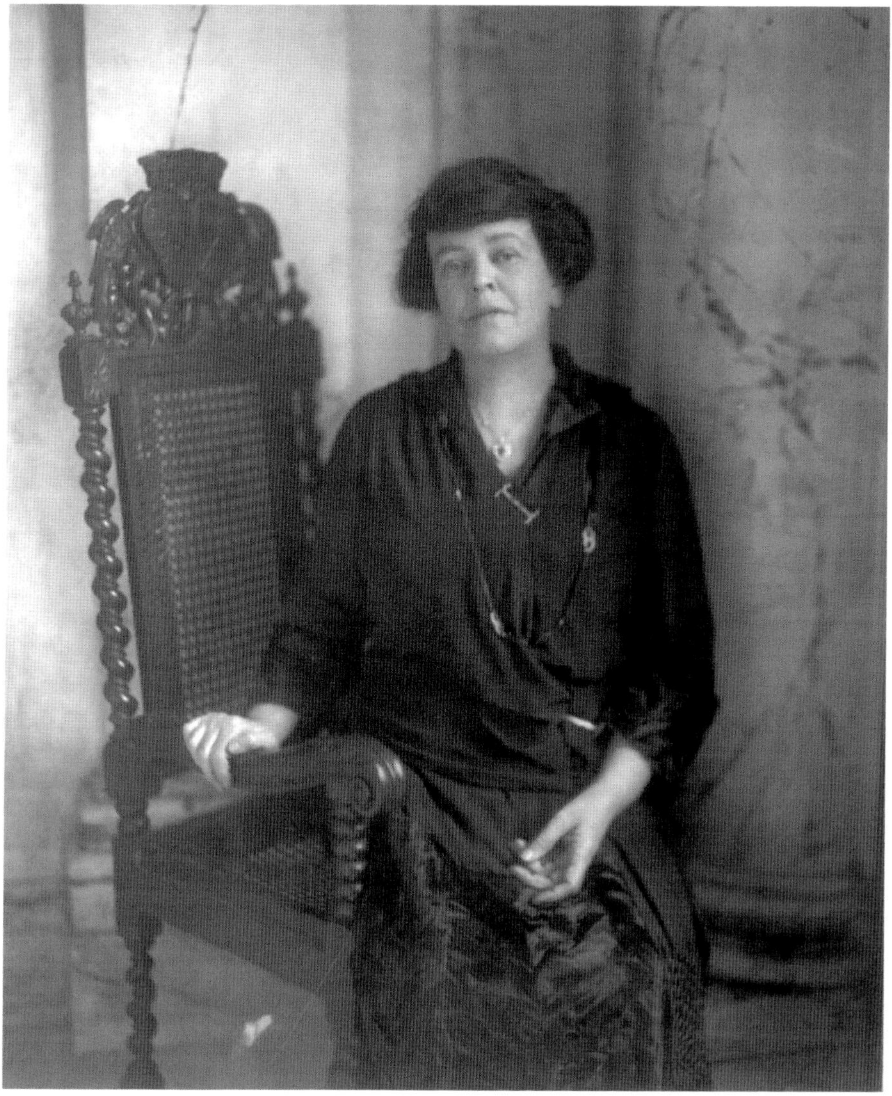

Alva Vanderbilt Belmont, suffragette and owner of Marble House in Newport, Rhode Island, circa 1910. *Courtesy of the Library of Congress.*

the love of Alva's life, and their legendary parties at Belcourt Castle were by far the most elaborate ever witnessed by New York society. When Oliver died suddenly in 1908 at the age of fifty, Alva was shattered.

Turning her grief into action, she threw herself headlong into the women's suffrage movement, attending conferences in London and New York and

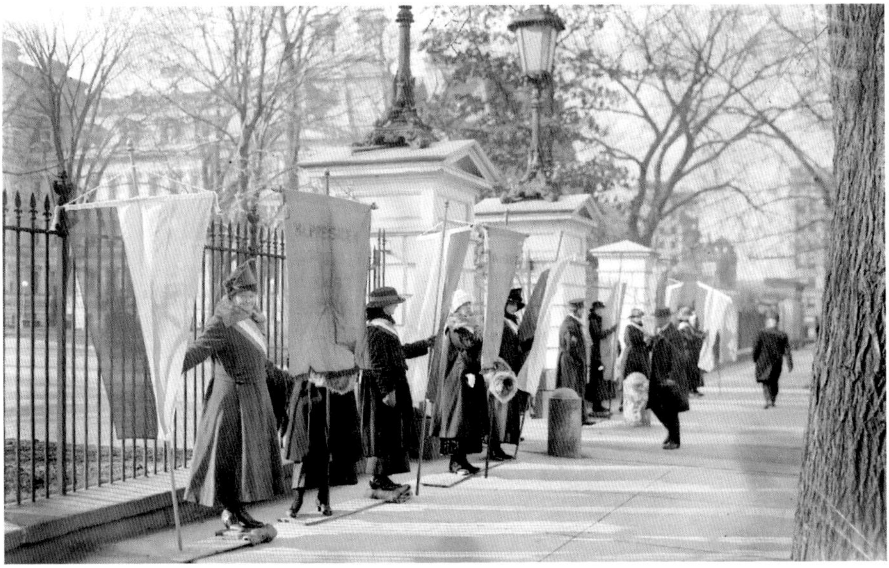

Alice Paul's suffragette movement, which Margaret supported, involved direct means of protesting the lack of women's rights, such as leading a march on the White House in 1914. *Courtesy of the Library of Congress.*

financing a suffrage office on Fifth Avenue in New York City. Alva organized the Women's Vote Parade in New York, leading fifty thousand women and their supporters down Fifth Avenue to Washington Square. She founded the Political Equity League and, with her friend Margaret, became involved in the National Women's Trade Union League, an important organization in the battle to reform women's working conditions in the early twentieth century that supported the right for women to unionize and fought to eliminate sweatshop conditions throughout America.

The two women traveled across the country, lecturing and writing articles in support of an eight-hour day and minimum wage for American workers (both male and female), affordable child care and the rights of women and minorities. It was Alva who encouraged Margaret to run for political office in 1914 as a candidate for the U.S. Senate. On a prosuffrage platform, Margaret represented the ideal that true change would only come when women had the right to vote and hold political office.

Another strong supporter of Margaret's candidacy was her dear friend from Denver, Judge Benjamin Barr Lindsey. Judge Lindsey was best known for establishing the first juvenile justice system in Denver, one that was so successful that it would eventually become the model adopted throughout the United States. In an era that saw boys and girls working in factories as young as age ten, Lindsey was also a pioneer in the movement to abolish child labor, believing that a workforce composed of children under the age of sixteen deprived them of their childhood and their ability to attend school and that no child should be subjugated to work that was mentally, physically or morally dangerous and harmful to the welfare of the child.

Margaret had met Judge Lindsey while living in Denver in 1903 and had immediately joined forces with him to champion these causes. Through her association with Lindsey, Margaret became even more adept at managing the press and, through free media, bringing attention to social issues to facilitate change. She became more politically active and, most importantly, evolved into an effective campaigner and fundraiser. Together, they formed the Juvenile Association for the Protection and Betterment of Children, and the association's annual benefits hosted by Margaret raised tens of thousands of dollars over the years for Judge Lindsey's projects, including a day nursery for impoverished children, public playgrounds and, most notably, the facilities that were built to help reform young boys brought to Judge Lindsey's court. Lindsey was well known to give a boy a "second chance" and tried to avoid sending one to prison, which Lindsey believed would be akin to sending the child into a "school for crime—deliberately teaching them to be horse thieves and safecrackers." Instead, Lindsey would refer boys to juvenile detention homes designed to Lindsey's specifications (and constructed with the use of funds raised by Mrs. J.J. Brown), where the boys would be taught skills to help them navigate young adulthood and, it was hoped, make them into more productive citizens after their release. Judge Lindsey would be a close friend and confidant of Margaret's throughout her life.

Alice Paul and the women of the Congressional Union also took up Margaret's Senate campaign. Her nomination was endorsed by Harriet Burton Laidlaw, president of the National Woman Suffrage Association of New York. Her Newport associates convinced the Rhode Island Suffrage Association to also endorse Margaret's campaign. Although residents of the state of Colorado had, by popular referendum, given women the right to vote in 1893, suffragists in Colorado still working for full suffrage across the United States also threw their support behind Margaret's candidacy.

However, fate would intervene. On June 28, 1914, Archduke Franz Ferdinand of Austria was assassinated, sparking the beginning of World War I. Moreover, a few weeks later, Margaret's sister Helen, who had married the Baron von Reitzenstein of Germany, telegrammed Margaret explaining that her husband had been summoned to the front by Emperor

Wilhelm. Margaret realized that it would not be acceptable for a U.S. senator to have a brother-in-law with a position on the kaiser's staff, and after seeking the council of her trusted allies, she was advised to withdraw her name from consideration.

Although she refrained from seeking political office in 1914, Margaret would continue to champion the rights of women, children and workers. She developed a series of lectures and spoke on many topics, not only those about social change in the United States but also of her experiences while traveling overseas and even of the writings of fellow Hannibalian Mark Twain. Margaret's lectures were well received, and she earned the reputation as an entertaining and effective public speaker. However, possibly due to her own personal experience of working in a factory at the age of thirteen, her most impassioned speeches were always on the rights of women and children.

Maggie Goes to Work

After young Maggie graduated from Mrs. O'Leary's grammar school, at age thirteen, she took a job at the nearby D.J. Garth & Bros. tobacco factory (formerly known as D.J. Garth & Company) on Palmyra Avenue. Each morning, a giant bell was rung at the facility, summoning Margaret and the other workers to their posts. "Almost the first that the writer can remember of Hannibal," wrote Thomas H. Bacon in 1905, "was [Garth's] silvery infallible bell long before day in the chill March mornings. Those were flush times in Hannibal. In the tobacco factories the boys could make remarkable wages."

John Garth's mansion was near the south end of Millionaires' Row on Fifth Street (his country estate, Woodside, was even larger and just three miles outside of Hannibal). The Garth tobacco processing factory had been founded by his father, John, in 1844, who was joined in business by his two sons, John and David, before the Civil War. With the outbreak of the war, the business was temporarily relocated to New York but was resumed in Hannibal in 1871. By the time Margaret was employed at Garth in 1880, the operation had grown to nearly one thousand employees. The enormous four-story manufacturing facility processed more than 500,000 pounds of tobacco per year.

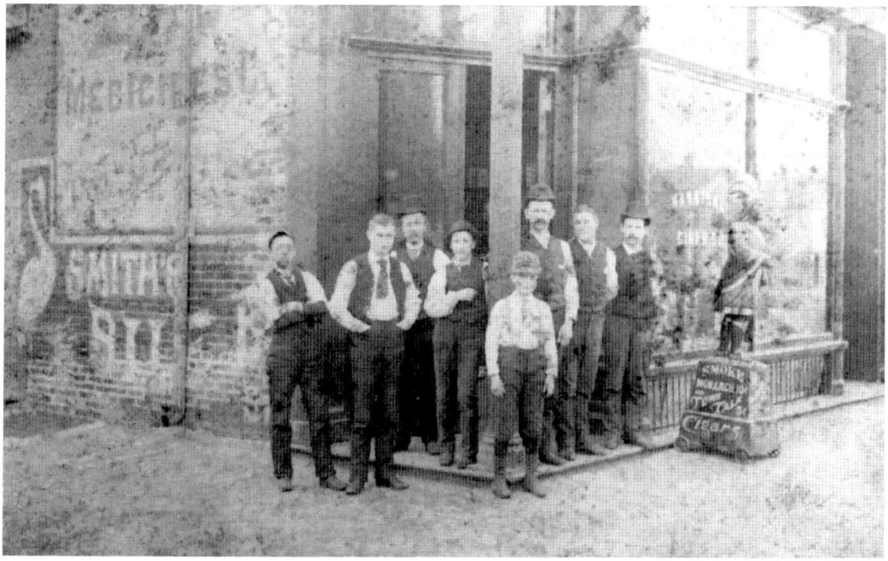

Storefront of the Hannibal Cigar Company, located at 601 Broadway, circa 1890. Tobacco processing and cigar making were major industries in Missouri throughout the second half of the 1800s and into the early 1900s. *Courtesy of Steve Chou.*

By 1885, Missouri was one of the leading manufacturers of cigars. There were 576 factories in Missouri, 62 percent of them located in St. Louis. Most were small, with fewer than ten employees; Garth's large operation was the exception, not the rule. Garth & Company was responsible for not only rolling cigars but also processing the raw tobacco leaves and wholesaling the processed tobacco to many of the small cigar rolling facilities in the region. Garth also supplied wholesalers, jobbers and retailers with private label brand cigars rolled at his facility. Tobacco use in the United States was enormous; some 6 billion cigars were consumed between 1880 and 1890, and taxes on tobacco accounted for one-third of all annual federal revenues collected at that time.

The larger tobacco firms in the United States were staffed predominantly by women. Particularly in the processing of tobacco, women's small hands were better for stripping the dried, parchment-like leaves from the prickly stems on the tobacco plants. This is most likely the job that Margaret would have been assigned to do. Factories such as these regularly scheduled their staff to work twelve-hour shifts six days per week. The cigar rollers, usually men, were the highest paid due to the skill involved; they would receive as much as two dollars per day. Women were paid much less, usually just over one dollar per day. Factories were quick to employ the less expensive female workers for all but the most skilled positions to keep overhead costs low.

All grown up with her own job at age thirteen, Maggie requested that her family begin to refer to her only as Margaret. There is no record of how long young Margaret worked at D.J. Garth & Bros. She never spoke of her experiences while working in the factory, and unlike her mother, who enjoyed her pipe, she was never known to have taken up the habit of smoking. There is, however, no question that Margaret did not intend to make her life's work stripping tobacco leaves from their stems.

The Home of the Friendless

In June 1880, Hannibal's Home of the Friendless opened in a new location just one block from Margaret's home on Denkler's Alley at 501 North Sixth Street. (This location would later become the site of Pettibone School.) The Home of the Friendless would replace the City Hospital for the indigent, established to serve the needs of transient, "respectable" women and children who needed a temporary shelter until they could once again become independent. Men were given temporary housing in Hannibal's Calaboose, a four-room stone building at the water's edge near the Hannibal Bridge that was also previously used as the city's jail and, on occasion, to retain livestock that had gone astray; there were no accommodations at the Calaboose for women and children, however, and a facility dedicated to their well-being was necessary.

Hannibal's *Morning Journal* of October 24, 1888, described the Home:

> *The Home is a substantial brick house on the corner of Sixth and Rock streets, on the crown of the bluff. It has a well-kept, large lawn. There is a brick walk from the street to the door of the house. There are five large rooms on the first floor, as yet unfurnished. The second floor has a reception room, folding doors opening from it into the matron's living room, and there are eight other rooms on the second floor, including a kitchen, dining room and six bedrooms. The third floor contains the boys' quarters and four sleeping apartments. Since the Home opened, a total of 510 people have been cared for there, mothers left alone in the world, fatherless and abused children, and the elderly. In most cases, 3 or 4 children come from the same family. The oldest inmate is Grandma Roberts, aged 85.*

The Home of the Friendless served the community for almost eighty years. Initially, it was supported entirely through donations from the kindhearted and gifts from the various civic and fraternal organizations in Hannibal. Prominent "society" women in Hannibal were named to the Home's board of directors and supervised the affairs of the home. The citizens of Hannibal were found to be very supportive of the Home. Churches sponsored charitable events to raise money, and different groups or clubs organized clothing drives and campaigns to finance special needs when they arose. The ladies on the Home's board sold yearly subscriptions for perpetual giving among their wealthy counterparts. To cheer the "inmates," as they were referred, some organizations would provide Christmas parties or other celebrations. Food drives were also held; one year, the school children of Hannibal held "Potato Day"—all children were asked to bring a potato with them to school to help feed the inmates at the Home.

Although Margaret Tobin did not record her activities during her time in Hannibal, it is certain that she was part of a community that was generous and encouraged volunteerism to care for those less fortunate. The Catholic faith has always been known for its charity and giving, and Margaret demonstrated throughout her life that she was a devout Catholic. It is not known how many of Hannibal's Irish participated in "Potato Day" for the Home of the Friendless, but it is certainly likely that Margaret and her family would have been sympathetic to the plight of those seeking shelter just one block from their home and would have joined with their community to assist those in need. To witness as a young girl the implementation of this type of social safety net would inspire Margaret to put forth similar efforts throughout her life. She would be recognized for her tireless devotion to these causes, offering aid to those in need each time the situation presented itself, not only in Leadville's mining camps, Denver's urban neighborhoods and at sea aboard *Carpathia* but also to those who resided in the countryside of war-ravaged France.

Part IV

Margaret Goes to War

In 1914, Margaret's son Lawrence, whose telegram had prompted his mother to board *Titanic*, was being sued for divorce. According to his wife, Eileen, Lawrence was a philanderer and ne'er-do-well. Indeed, Lawrence demonstrated difficulty in settling into any sort of a career, and although J.J. grumbled in letters he wrote to Lawrence about his apparent unwillingness to hold a job or inability to maintain his focus on anything for very long, he continued to financially support his son throughout his life.

Margaret was very upset at the thought of one of her children divorcing. She decided to intervene and visited Lawrence in Golden, Colorado, where he had enrolled in the Colorado School of Mines. Her persuasions came to no avail; Lawrence and Eileen legally divorced in July 1915. Margaret was worried of the effect this might have on her grandchildren, Lawrence Jr. (whom they called "Pat") and little Elizabeth ("Bettie"), just shy of two years old.

However, once again, events in Europe would intervene. After the United States entered into World War I in 1917, Lawrence announced that he would be joining the fight, leaving the School of Mines after attending only two semesters. Shortly before being shipped out, he and Eileen reconciled and remarried. The entire family, including Margaret and J.J., were present in New York to see Lawrence off as he made his way to France in uniform.

When war was declared, Margaret's first response was to offer Mon Etui to the Newport office of the American Red Cross as a hospital and rehabilitation facility, which she would furnish and equip at her own expense.

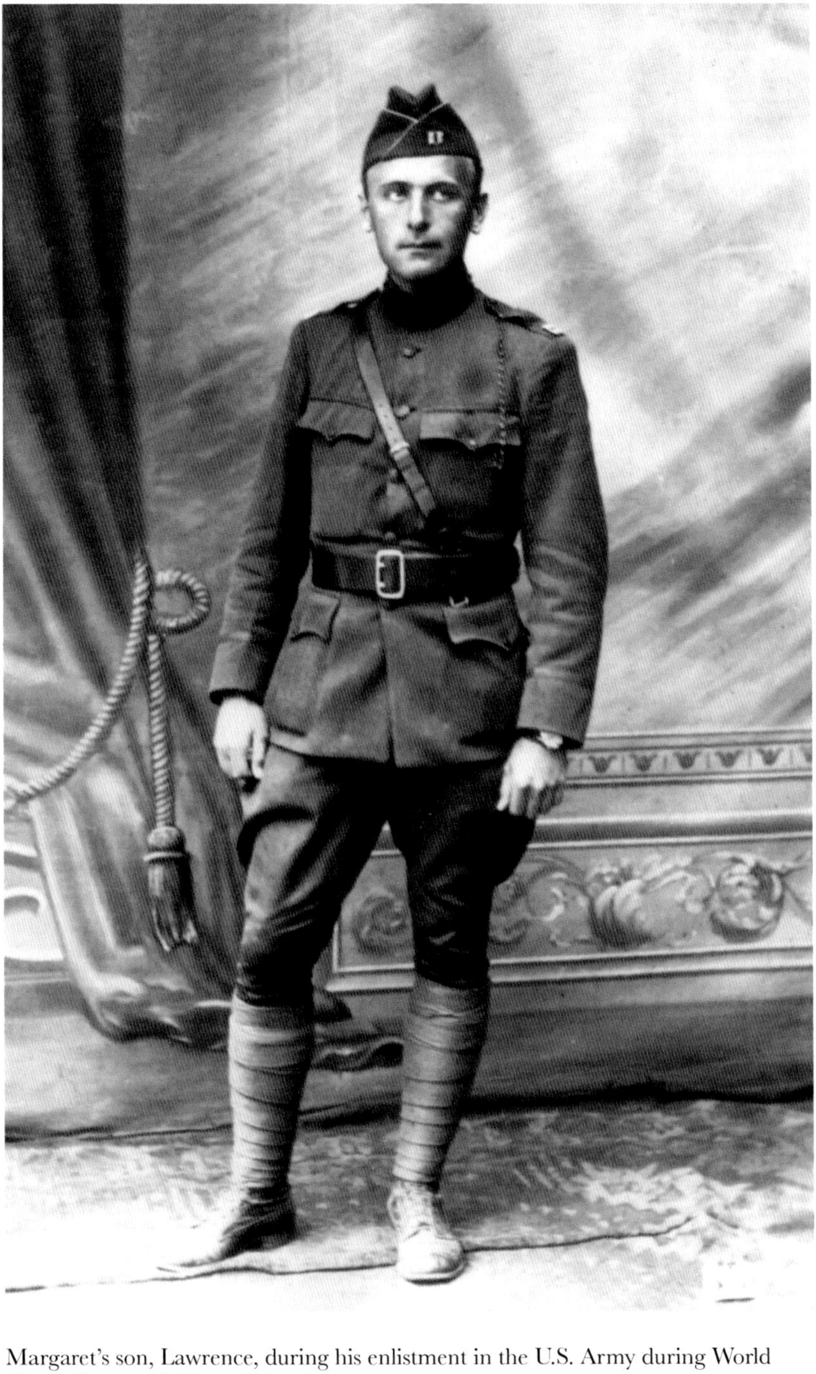

Margaret's son, Lawrence, during his enlistment in the U.S. Army during World War I. *Courtesy of History Colorado.*

Next, after gathering medical equipment and recruiting nurses to join her, Margaret set sail for France. "If I were requested to personify perpetual activity," one New York reporter declared, "I believe I'd name Mrs. James J. Brown, the Newport social figure, suffragette, patriot."

Anne Murray Dike and Anne Morgan, a friend of Margaret's and the daughter of tycoon J.P. Morgan, established the American Committee for Devastated France in 1919, commonly referred to as CARD (the acronym is for the French translation, *Comité Américain des Régions Dévastées*). Its purpose was to assist the French in their recovery efforts after the destruction they suffered during the war by rebuilding homes, setting up hospitals and raising funds for assistance. Dike, a physician, set up the headquarters for CARD in the seventeenth-century Chateau de Blerancourt, 110 miles north of Paris and less than 40 miles from the war's front. Margaret was eager to join in this effort.

"We do not want sightseers who would like to go over for half a year to view France's battlefields," Anne Morgan said to the *New York Times*. Most volunteers working for CARD were wealthy American women such as Margaret, as they were required to be able to speak French, hold a driver's license so they could be relied on to drive ambulances and pay for their own uniforms and personal expenses, which could reach $1,500 for a six-month tour of duty. The ladies worked long hours and lived in sparsely furnished barracks. Many of the volunteers were female physicians who, after being denied the opportunity to serve alongside men in the U.S. military medical corps, were provided the chance to practice their profession as members of CARD.

Margaret was named one of the directors of CARD and worked with the government and local residents to rebuild homes, schools and medical facilities and to distribute food, clothing and household supplies. Health education was provided to the townsfolk, and crops were planted with donated seed. CARD also provided entertainment and cultural activities to brighten the lives of villagers who suffered many dark years during the war.

After the war ended, Anne Morgan and Anne Murray Dike transformed the Chateau de Blerancourt into the Museum of Franco-American Cooperation. The museum houses an impressive art collection, special exhibitions featuring treasured artifacts and extensive documentation that tells the story of the humanitarian aid provided to France by the United States during the Great War and of the Franco-American relationship fostered during that era. (Since World War II, the collection has expanded to encompass three hundred years of cooperation between the two countries.) Today, one visiting the museum will find an engraved plaque on prominent display that recognizes those individuals who were the major benefactors of the museum; among those listed, you will find the name Margaret Tobin Brown.

Americans, particularly women, found new freedoms in France. The Left Bank attracted many expatriates to its shore because of the more liberal French social norms, and women, such as Gertrude Stein and Josephine Baker, led lives in France that they would never have had the opportunity to live in the United States. The war brought many American women overseas to assist in relief programs, but once they arrived and were witness to this newfound attitude toward women, many stayed. France would be a second home to Margaret after the war, and she traveled back and forth across the North Atlantic throughout the 1920s. The French appreciated Margaret just as ardently; she was awarded the French Legion of Honor Medal in 1932 for her charitable efforts in France, particularly for her assistance during the Great War.

Lawrence survived World War I, although he was wounded after being exposed to mustard gas in November 1918. He was sent to London to recuperate under the supervision of the Astor family, and when honorably discharged on January 23, 1919, he was recognized for his service as a member of the unit that breached the Hindenburg line. When he returned to America, Lawrence, Eileen and their children resumed their lives together, taking up residence in Fort Collins, Colorado.

Margaret continued to volunteer her time and resources, assisting wounded American soldiers returning from the war. At Briar Cliff Lodge in New York, she worked with soldiers blinded in the war, helping them transition back into civilian life. Proudly revealing her connection to fellow Hannibalian Mark Twain, she facilitated the printing of a series of Twain's writings into braille and made them available to the wounded heroes.

Hannibal Ushers in a New Era for Women

Early on the morning of August 31, 1920, rain was falling in Hannibal. A determined twenty-six-year-old woman set out to walk fifteen muddy blocks. She was on a very special mission. Accompanying her was her husband, Morris Byrum, Hannibal's city clerk.

When the couple reached their destination, they were met by Morris's father, Lacey Byrum. A special election was being held that day to fill a vacancy on the Hannibal City Council, and Lacey Byrum was serving as the Democratic election judge. With a premonition that this might be a momentous occasion, the elder Mr. Byrum suggested that his daughter-in-law, Marie Rouff Byrum, appear at the polling place no later than 7:00 a.m. to cast her ballot.

As Marie slipped her vote into the ballot box, she became the very first woman to vote in the United States after passage of the Nineteenth Amendment to the United States Constitution. The amendment had been ratified just two weeks earlier on August 18, 1920. Her vote fulfilled the dreams of women suffragists across the country and ushered in a new chapter of American history.

Margaret Tobin Brown must have swelled with pride when she learned that the first vote cast by a woman took place in her beloved hometown of Hannibal.

"Look After Your Mother"

When J.J. and Margaret separated in 1909, one of her complaints was that he seemed to be a hypochondriac. Constantly complaining of one ailment or another, perhaps from the stress of the workload that he put himself under, J.J. never admitted to feeling healthy. He suffered a slight stroke in 1913 that alarmed everyone in the family, including Margaret, but he recovered. However, his health was a constant concern, particularly to Helen, who took over the task of seeing to it that her father was taking good care of himself. After the stroke, J.J. frequently checked into hospitals or was cared for in private hotels.

By 1920, J.J.'s health had seriously deteriorated. Now in his sixties, the welfare of his children and grandchildren was his primary concern, even more so than his business dealings. He became melancholy. "I thought away back in the past and of all the sacrifices made for others, and that at last, it should come to this," J.J. wrote to Helen. "No family, home, or friends, all alone in a dingy old room…you were young, your Brother was young, but your Mother carried you off and away among strangers while I was in the Hills delving for some thing to make a home and a living. Now you are in New York and your mother is Hellknowswhere, spending her money."

In 1921, J.J. was hospitalized in Los Angeles and sent an urgent telegram to Helen, beckoning her to come and care for him. Helen remained at his side for six weeks, finally convincing him that she needed to return to her family and for J.J. to accompany her back to New York. They made a stop in Colorado to visit friends in both Denver and Leadville, but by the time they arrived in New York, J.J.'s condition had worsened. Lawrence received a telegram regarding his father's condition.

Lawrence was now living alone in LaJolla, California, where he assisted in producing silent films with John Gorman Pictures. Here he met and married his second wife, silent film star Mildred Gregory. After receiving the telegram, Lawrence made the decision to remain in California.

By the first of September, J.J. was admitted to Nassau Hospital for testing. While hospitalized, he suffered a series of heart attacks. As Helen prepared to leave the hospital to return home to rest on the night of September 4, J.J. turned to her and said, "Look after your mother."

J.J. Brown died on the morning of September 5, 1922. He was alone at the time of his passing, as Helen did not reach the hospital in time, arriving twenty minutes too late.

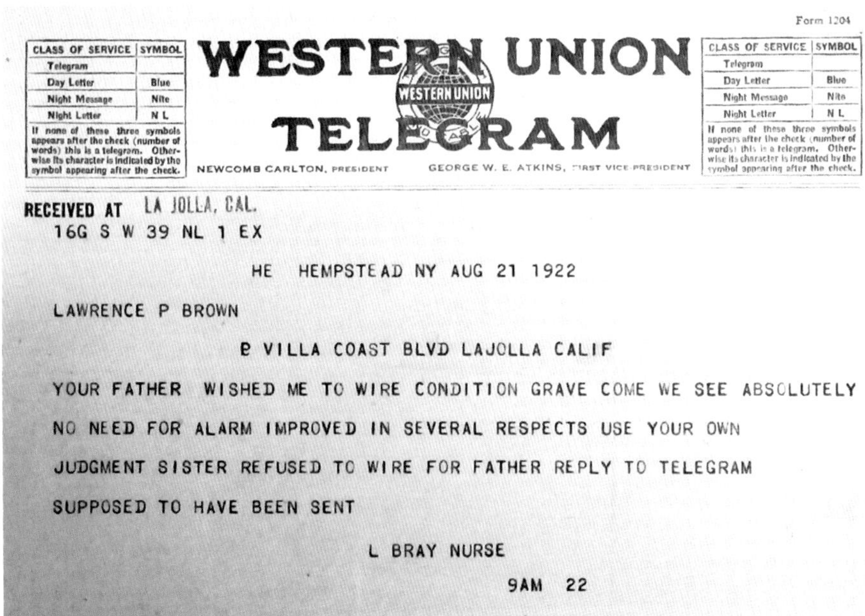

Form 1204

CLASS OF SERVICE	SYMBOL
Telegram	
Day Letter	Blue
Night Message	Nite
Night Letter	N L

If none of these three symbols appears after the check (number of words) this is a telegram. Otherwise its character is indicated by the symbol appearing after the check.

WESTERN UNION TELEGRAM

NEWCOMB CARLTON, PRESIDENT GEORGE W. E. ATKINS, FIRST VICE-PRESIDENT

CLASS OF SERVICE	SYMBOL
Telegram	
Day Letter	Blue
Night Message	Nite
Night Letter	N L

If none of these three symbols appears after the check (number of words) this is a telegram. Otherwise its character is indicated by the symbol appearing after the check.

RECEIVED AT LA JOLLA, CAL.

16G S W 39 NL 1 EX

HE HEMPSTEAD NY AUG 21 1922

LAWRENCE P BROWN

8 VILLA COAST BLVD LAJOLLA CALIF

YOUR FATHER WISHED ME TO WIRE CONDITION GRAVE COME WE SEE ABSOLUTELY NO NEED FOR ALARM IMPROVED IN SEVERAL RESPECTS USE YOUR OWN JUDGMENT SISTER REFUSED TO WIRE FOR FATHER REPLY TO TELEGRAM SUPPOSED TO HAVE BEEN SENT

L BRAY NURSE

9AM 22

Telegram sent to Lawrence about his father's deteriorating health, August 1922. *Courtesy of Denver Public Library.*

When word of J.J. Brown's death was received in Colorado, the *Denver Post* contacted Margaret and asked her to comment:

> *Let me say here that I've been all over the world. I have known more or less intimately the greatest people in the world from Kings down, or up, as one cares to view them, and I've never met a finer, bigger, more worthwhile man than J.J. Brown. In spite of certain qualities of our natures which made companionship impossible between us, I salute his memory and claim him to have been without a peer.*

Part V

Dreaming of a Different Life

Although Margaret would have worked long hours hunched over stacks of tobacco leaves at D.J. Garth & Bros., she was earning a wage and, although money was tight, certainly would have reserved a small portion for discretionary spending. Her love of music and theater was evident all her life, and it is likely that she would have indulged in tickets to the many theatrical events prevalent in Hannibal during her teenage years. Operas, orchestras, vaudeville troupes, old-timey minstrel shows, circuses and other fantastic performances were regularly scheduled in Hannibal. The town's modern rail service allowed the largest circuses to come to town; railroads, particularly the Shortline, offered special excursions attracting those from outlying towns to come and enjoy the performances. The circus parades were always eagerly anticipated, provided free to the community by the circus promoters to entice residents to see the show. Some promoters, such as the Lemon Brothers, Barnum & Bailey and Wallace and Hagenbeck, would have their entire circus represented, with some parades lasting up to three hours, closing down traffic on Broadway and Main Street as hordes of onlookers crowded the streets. It must have been quite a sight to see a parade of elephants marching down Main Street in downtown Hannibal.

In 1882, fifteen-year-old Margaret would have taken great delight spending an evening attending a theatrical event at the newly constructed Park Theater. In their book *The Story of Hannibal*, written for the U.S. bicentennial in 1976, Hannibal historians J. Hurley and Roberta Hagood described the Park Theater:

> *The Park Theatre on Fifth and Center, built in 1882, attracted nationally known musicians, entertainers, lecturers, actors and performers. Hannibal, a railroad center between Chicago and St. Louis and Chicago and Kansas City, was a convenient stop-over for troupes traveling by train. The excellent theater facilities and the outstanding support given by the citizenry made Hannibal a favorite place for entertainers. The opening production at the Park Theater was a play,* Hazel and Kirk. *The stage and dressing rooms were more than adequate for the times. A stage 65 feet long, 45 feet deep, and 60 feet to the rigging loft allowed as many as 48 drops of curtain scenery to be installed at one time. It was ornately decorated in blue and gold. An orchestra pit was located directly in front of the stage. The interior of the theatre was elaborately aggrandized. It seated 1,100 patrons. The first ten rows, known as the dress circle, were occupied by the wealthiest patrons. The dress circle was separated from the rest of the main floor by a velvet-topped partition. The first row was commonly known as the "bald-headed row" because so many wealthy bald headed men sat there. Two private boxes adjoining the sides of the stage were used by special guests who wish to view and be viewed. The theater had two balconies; the upper known as the gallery had less expensive seats and its patrons were sometimes noisy and impolite. A policeman usually stood in the gallery to control this part of the clientele. The theater was steam heated and lighted by gaslights.*

To house these entertainers and other dignitaries who made their way to Hannibal, the famous Park Hotel was built overlooking Central Park at the corner of Center and Fourth Streets, one block across the park from where the Park Theater was built and just five blocks from the Tobin household. The magnificent Second Empire structure featured three stories, topped with a mansard roof that comprised its fourth floor. Built by J.B. Price and Company at a cost of more than $75,000, the hotel featured exquisite lobbies, private salons and parlors and a thirty-six- by sixty-three-foot dining room.

Fictional accounts of Margaret's life, published after her death by authors such as Gene Fowler and Caroline Bancroft, invented the tale that Margaret left the tobacco factory to work as a waitress at the Park Hotel. According to the legend, one fateful day, she begged to be assigned to wait on Mark Twain, who was supposedly visiting Hannibal while writing a new book and taking lunch at the Park Hotel dining room. Twain waxed poetically about the West, telling tales of his adventures in Nevada and California, and

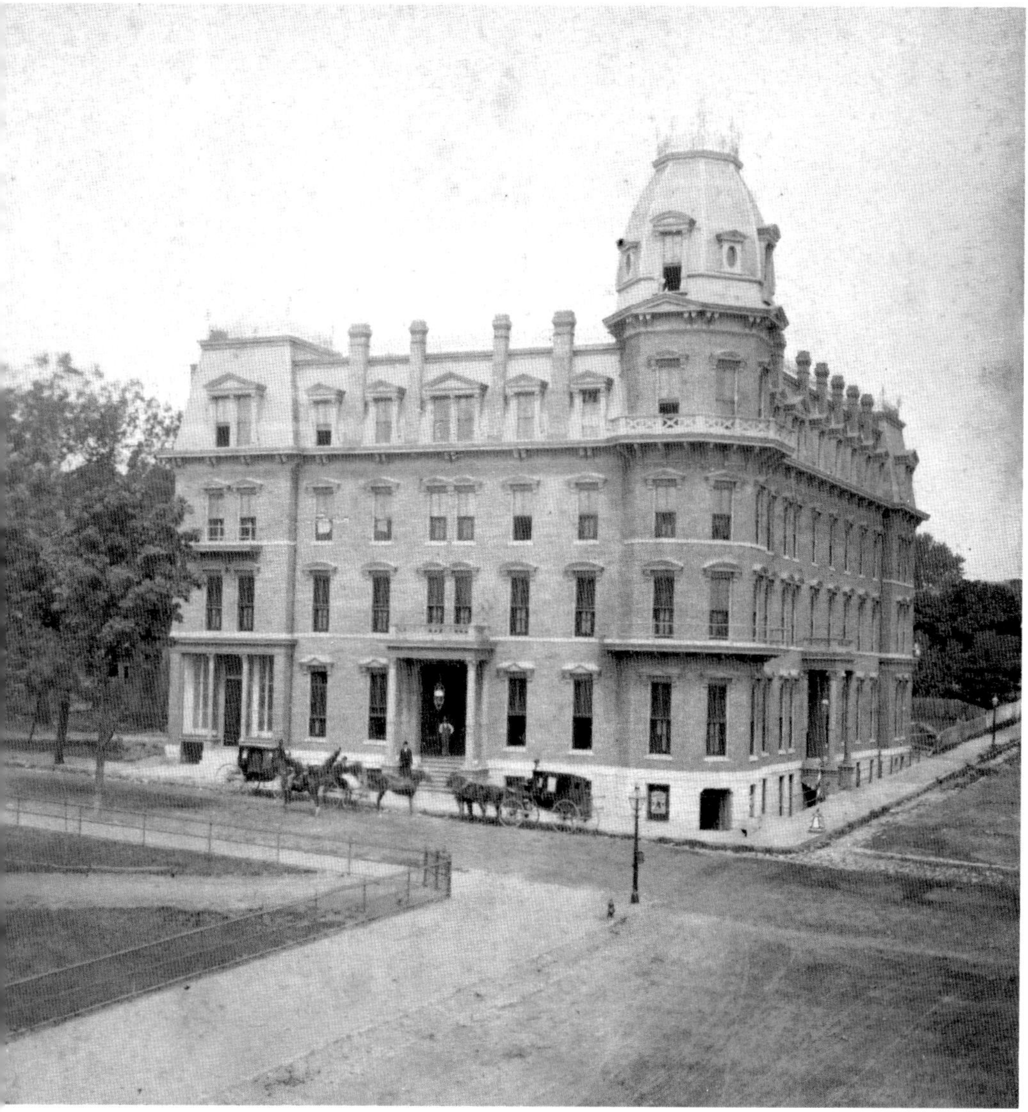

Hannibal's elegant Park Hotel overlooking Central Park at the corner of Fourth and Center Streets, circa 1885. *Courtesy of Steve Chou.*

encouraged Margaret to seek a new life out west in a place such as the gold mines of Leadville, Colorado.

In the biography of Margaret Tobin Brown, *Molly Brown: Unravelling the Myth*, Kristen Iversen debunked this fairytale:

> *The Park Hotel did exist in Hannibal and indeed was very reputable during the 1870s and 1880s* [the Park Hotel was razed by fire on April 27, 1899]. *One interesting overlooked fact, however, is that*

> *the hotel hired only male waiters for its formal dining room and almost certainly would not have hired an Irish girl at the time, except perhaps as a housemaid. Samuel Clemens, not yet known as Mark Twain, left Hannibal in 1853 at the age of seventeen—fourteen years before Margaret Tobin was born. Years later he did return to Hannibal during his 1868 and 1869 lecture tour; however, he never stayed at the hotel but rather put up at the six-hundred-acre, sprawling Victorian-style mansion owned by the Garth family* [Garth's Woodside estate], *with whom he was good friends. He visited Hannibal again in 1885, just before Margaret left for Leadville, but it seems unlikely that they met.*

Being Irish, being Catholic, being *female*, there were limited opportunities for Margaret to improve her situation in Hannibal. She would undoubtedly marry a fellow Catholic, probably an Irishman, raise a family and live in a modest home near her family. At some point, Margaret decided that she had other ideas in mind. She wanted to make a way in the world that would ease the burden of her father, a man she adored. "I longed to be rich enough to give him a home so that he would not have to work," Margaret said many years later. She knew that this would not be likely if she were to stay in Hannibal; there is little doubt that if Margaret had remained in Hannibal, she would have been assured a very different life than the one she ultimately led.

Margaret's elder half-sister, Mary Ann, had married Jack Landrigan, a blacksmith in Hannibal. He was convinced that greater opportunities were to be found in Colorado, and in 1883, Jack, Mary Ann and her brother Daniel headed to the burgeoning mining community of Leadville. Once there, Jack set up a blacksmith shop at 529 East Fifth Street, and Mary Ann found herself with child, the first of their eleven children. Daniel made a home for himself at 722 East Fifth Street, just two blocks up from the Landrigans. In early spring 1886, he wired money back to Hannibal so that his two sisters, Margaret and Helen, could come for a visit.

When Margaret packed for this trip, she was not planning to return. Helen, only fifteen, would return to Hannibal, but Margaret, now eighteen, knew that this was her chance. The Tobin family walked the two teenage girls through town to the south side of Main Street and waited for the train to arrive under one of the long, covered platforms of Union Depot.

While possibly seen as a gamble to Hannibalians (a boomtown such as Leadville that grows quickly can die just as quickly), Margaret was eager to begin her thrilling new life in Colorado. True, Hannibal was a stable, more

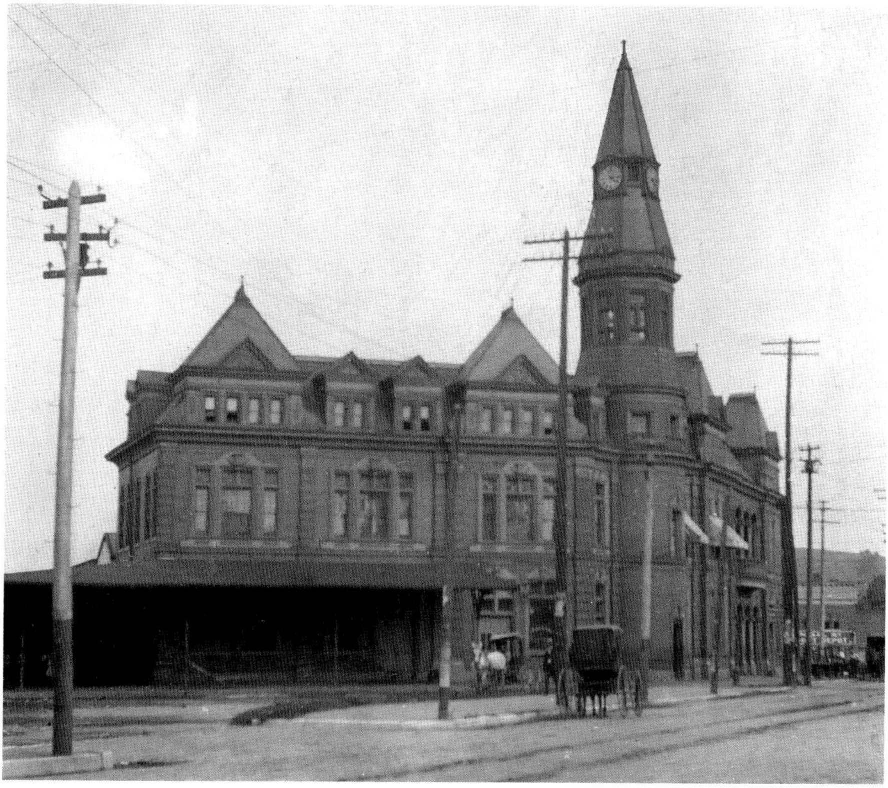

Hannibal's Union Depot on South Main Street, completed in 1882, would see thirty-five to fifty trains from six railroad lines pass through daily by the 1890s. *Courtesy of Steve Chou.*

economically diverse city than Leadville, which would feel comfortable for some, but Margaret had lived through enough hardships and had decided long before boarding the train to Leadville that she would not settle for the same struggles as her parents. She wanted to bring wealth to the family, and while Leadville carried no guarantees, its possibilities outweighed the limiting certainties of her hometown.

Completed just four years earlier in 1882, Hannibal's Union Depot was now a landmark in town, an ornate, three-story limestone structure surmounted with a clock tower to help keep passengers on time. The upper floors, where guests could stay overnight in one of twenty-two hotel rooms, were open in the center and illuminated by a massive central skylight. The first-floor waiting room, exquisitely appointed with fine woodwork from nearby craftsmen, was used primarily by men, as there were spittoons placed in strategic locations on the decorative tile floors. A separate, smaller waiting room was provided for women, the benches resembling church pews fashioned of sturdy, quarter-sawn oak. Adjacent to the waiting rooms was a newsstand and lunch counter; for those with more time to spare, a dining room was located in the southeast corner of the building that could be cordoned off for meetings. The indoor plumbing was modern for its time, and the entire building was kept warm in the winter by steam-filled, decorative radiators. Margaret would make her way through Union Depot many times throughout the course of her life.

However, in the spring of 1886, on this, her very first trip, Margaret waved goodbye to her Hannibal family as the train slowly pulled away from Union Depot. She was eager to begin her new life and stake her own claim in the mountains of Colorado.

Part VI

On the Road to Riches

Although Hannibal bustled and churned like the grinding wheels of a steam-powered locomotive in its continuous surge of industrialism, the town looked mild-mannered and disciplined compared to the Rocky Mountain free-for-all that was Leadville, Colorado. By the mid-1880s, the area had already experienced two floods, rushes of potential prospectors hoping to change or add to their fortunes by picking and boring their way through the mountain range. The first rush to the area actually predated Leadville itself in the early 1860s, with gold being discovered in what was called California Gulch. After millions of dollars' worth of gold were extracted from the earth, these claims ran dry by the mid-1860s. This did not stop a few hundred miners from continuing their quests, however, and by 1876–77, strains of lead carbonate ore had been found in a spot near the gulch. While lead did not come close to replacing gold in value, the lead ore could fulfill a variety of functions once smelted. More importantly, the ore also contained silver.

The discovery of silver turned the settlement area into a boomtown within a year, and the town of Leadville was created and incorporated in 1878. By 1880, Leadville could boast of having one of the largest silver mining encampments in the world, as its recorded population of nearly fifteen thousand didn't account for thousands who lived on their outlying claims; different accounts place the number anywhere from twenty-four thousand to forty thousand people in and around the brand-new community. Leadville had established itself as the second-largest city in Colorado, with hundreds

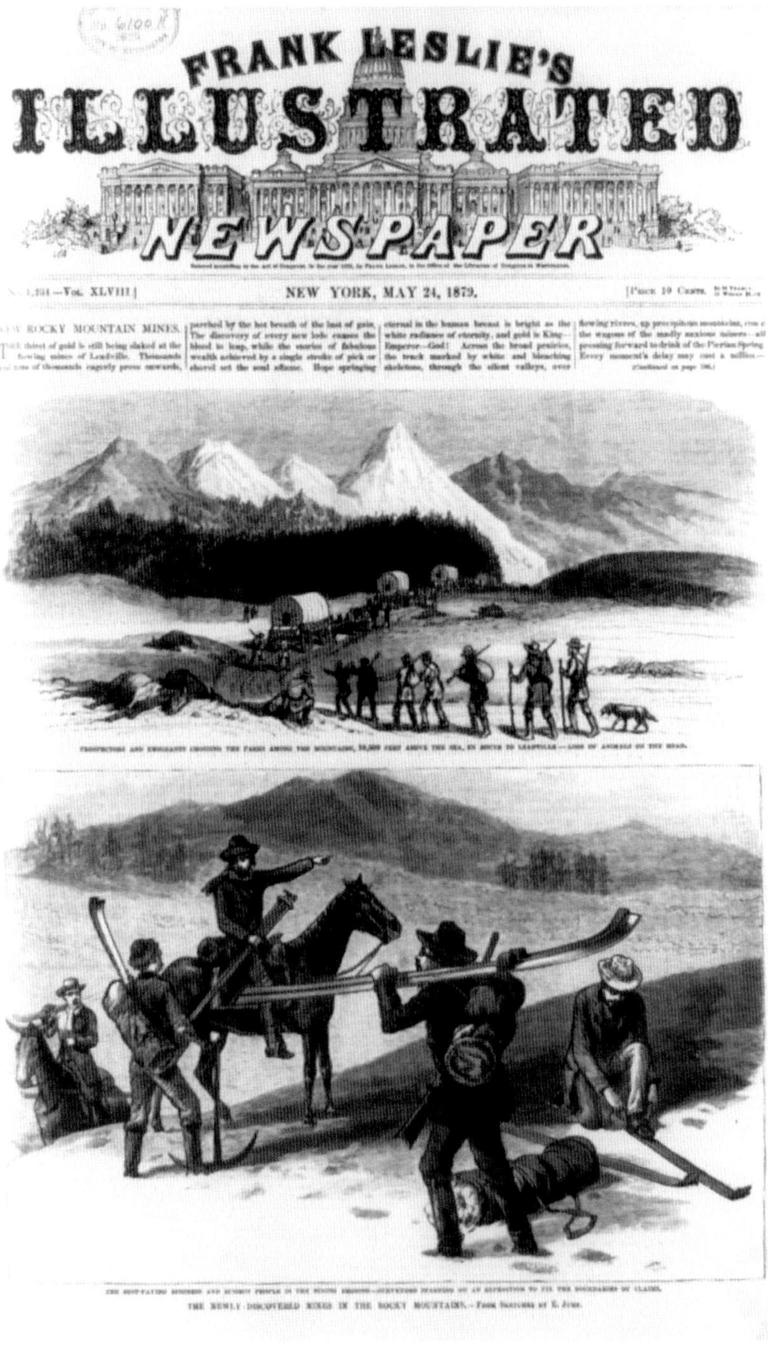

FRANK LESLIE'S ILLUSTRATED NEWSPAPER

No. 1,234—Vol. XLVIII.] NEW YORK, MAY 24, 1879. [Price 10 Cents.

ROCKY MOUNTAIN MINES.

THE thirst of gold is still being slaked at the flowing mines of Leadville. Thousands and tens of thousands eagerly press onwards, parched by the hot breath of the lust of gain. The discovery of every new lode causes the blood to leap, while the stories of fabulous wealth achieved by a single stroke of pick or shovel set the soul aflame. Hope springing eternal in the human breast is bright as the white radiance of eternity, and gold is King—Emperor—God! Across the broad prairies, the track marked by white and bleaching skeletons, through the silent valleys, over flowing rivers, up precipitous mountains, [illegible] the wagons of the madly anxious miners—all pressing forward to drink of the Pierian Spring. Every moment's delay may cost a million.—

(Continued on page [illegible].)

THE NEWLY-DISCOVERED MINES IN THE ROCKY MOUNTAINS.—From Sketches by E. Jump.

Articles such as the one in *Frank Leslie's Illustrated Newspaper* (1879) touted at length the fortunes awaiting those who ventured across the Rocky Mountains to Leadville. *Courtesy of the Library of Congress.*

of hopefuls a week slogging through rugged passes to reach the silver oasis situated more than 150 miles high up into the mountains above the larger city of Denver.

Margaret stepped off the Leadville train platform into an entirely different world compared to the one she'd left behind in Hannibal. This was the Wild West at its most clichéd—Leadville greeted its migrants with what seemed a near-chaotic cacophony of sounds, a circus-like atmosphere that continued around the clock. Freighters carrying ore barreled through the city all day, the dusty roadways sometimes clogged for a mile or longer with the traffic of men, mules and metal, all made possible through mining. The theaters, dance halls, casinos and saloons provided their share of noise throughout the night: the clinking of glass, the plinking of almost-in-tune pianos played by itinerant musicians and the dull roar of crowds sharing fellowship around the bar. With a city almost solely dependent on a narrow range of speculative industries for its success, the amount of wealth at stake affected the behavior of the residents. When some of the silver mines in the 1800s would garner $10,000 in revenue *per day*, the sheer amount of money flowing into and out of Leadville pushed some residents, drifters and squatters to extremes in order to get and keep their riches. They worked hard and they played hard, and in many instances, it was every man for himself.

Men outnumbered women three to one in Leadville, good odds for a young lady seeking matrimony. However, meeting suitable candidates was difficult, and constraints imposed by Victorian social norms limited the choices ladies would have to earn wages to sustain them until their wedding day. Margaret could have chosen to work as a maid, cook or laundress, serving as a domestic just as the Irish girls did back in Hannibal. One profession that Margaret did not pursue but would have fit her mission to marry a rich man was that of dance hall girl. Working in a dance hall would have given a young woman the greatest exposure to meeting a variety of single men; one never knew which of the seemingly lonely ne'er-do-well miners passing through the halls might at any time become rich overnight, and the girls would become prospectors themselves to mine for men who could provide them with a better life. As a last resort, some of the once-hopeful Leadville women had chosen the unthinkable and joined the ranks of "ladies of the evening." Margaret had moved to Leadville to create a new life and marry into wealth; regardless of how naïve that notion might have been, Leadville certainly provided the opportunity for this dream to become reality. Everyone arriving in Leadville dreamed of striking it rich, but there were many different pathways to choose, and not everyone would find gold at the end of their rainbow.

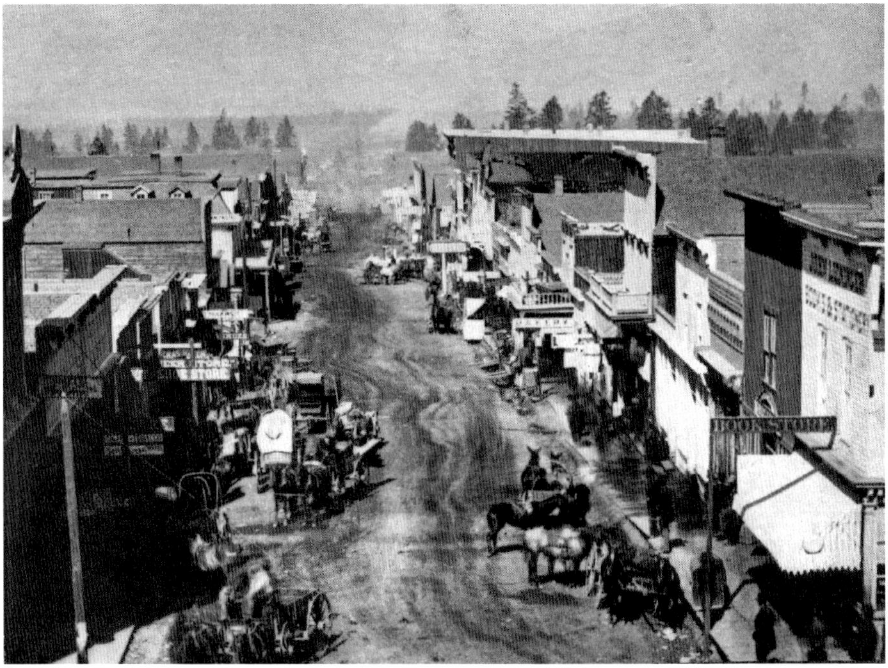

Within a year following this 1879 image of downtown Leadville, the town would swell to become the second-largest city in Colorado. *Courtesy of the Library of Congress.*

Upon her arrival in Leadville, Margaret moved in with her brother Daniel and kept house for him as he tried to break into the mining industry. She avoided the bawdy houses, saloons and dance halls and instead was hired as a seamstress at Daniels, Fisher & Smith, a small dry goods store on Harrison Avenue, where she sewed carpeting and draperies. (Although modest, this small store would one day grow into the corporation known as the May Company, owners of the Macy's and Marshall Field's department stores until 2006).

As would any respectable young Irish Catholic lady, Margaret soon became a member of the local parish in Leadville. Just west of downtown, at the corner of Seventh and Poplar Streets, the tall, thin spire of Annunciation Church was built to pierce the sky, a landmark seen by all of Leadville. Father Henry Robinson held the first mass at the new church on New Year's Day, 1880, just six years before Margaret's arrival. As it was with the Immaculate Conception parish in Hannibal, Annunciation was the epicenter of life for Leadville's burgeoning Irish Catholic community, and Margaret would find fellowship there with others of her faith.

The Irish in Leadville formed a large percentage of the predominantly immigrant community—nearly everyone in town was from Somewhere Else. Thus, there was even less discrimination for ethnic groups such as the Irish than there had been in Hannibal. Leadville truly provided to all men equally the chance to live the American dream; if you were ambitious and worked hard, there was nothing to restrain you from achieving your goals, regardless of your ethnicity or religious beliefs. The only thing that might prohibit you in your pursuit of the American dream was your gender.

Not long after her arrival in Leadville, in late May or early June 1886, Margaret attended a picnic hosted by the Annunciation parish with her family and new friends she'd made. Just as her parents had done some twenty-five years before her, Margaret was to meet her future husband at a church picnic.

James Joseph Brown was a handsome man. His demeanor matched his height; standing five feet, eleven inches, most remembered him as a towering figure. J.J., as he liked to be called, was quick to smile and had piercing blue eyes. He was intelligent and gregarious and, most of all, ambitious. To Margaret's dismay, however, he was not wealthy.

J.J. had been born to John and Cecilia Brown on September 27, 1855. John Brown, who had sailed from Ireland during the famine in 1848, had met Cecilia when she was teaching school in Wayne County, Pennsylvania. Young J.J. was educated at St. John's Academy in Pittson, Pennsylvania, and left home at the age of twenty-three to follow the allure of the gold and silver mines in the West. He made his way to Colorado after spending two years in the mines of South Dakota and settled in Leadville in 1882.

J.J. was a self-starter; each night, after a long day toiling in the mines of Eben Smith and David Moffat, the joint owners of several large mines in Leadville, he would study his books on mining by the glow of gaslight. Smith was impressed with young J.J.'s determination and regularly promoted him through the ranks. J.J. would eventually become the superintendent of the Maid and Henriette Mine, one of the largest mineral producers in Leadville. However, J.J. was still just a worker earning a wage—far from the rich man whom Margaret someday hoped to marry.

J.J. was instantly smitten with the feisty Margaret Tobin, she with her auburn hair and eyes that twinkled. In later years, Margaret said that she had found J.J. to be "irresistible" and "charming." Even if he was not wealthy, he was making a very good living in Leadville, and it would make her mother happy to know that he was Irish and Catholic.

They recognized a kindred spirit in each other, both believing that with hard work and determination they could make a good life for themselves.

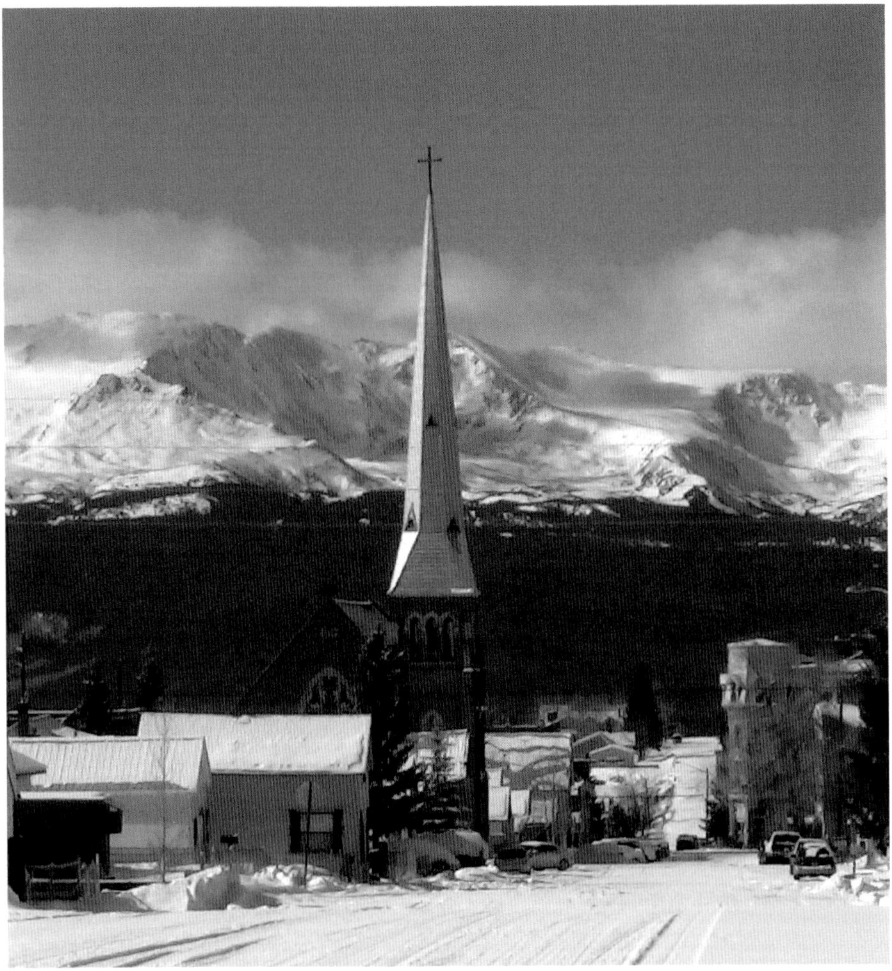

Margaret Tobin married James J. Brown at Annunciation Church in Leadville, Colorado, on September 1, 1886. *Photo by author.*

If they combined their energies, they would make a good team. Just three months after their introduction, J.J. and Margaret were married at Leadville's Annunciation Church by Father Robinson on September 1, 1886.

Many years later, Margaret explained her decision to marry J.J. Brown:

> *I wanted a rich man, but I loved Jim Brown. I thought about how I wanted comfort for my father and how I had determined to stay single until a man presented himself who could give to the tired old man the things I longed for him. Jim was as poor as we were, and had no better chance in*

> *life. I struggled hard with myself in those days. I loved Jim, but he was poor. Finally I decided that I'd be better off with a poor man whom I loved than with a wealthy one whose money had attracted me. So I married Jim Brown. I gave up cooking for my brother and moved to Jim's cabin, where the work was just as hard.*

Margaret left her job at the dry goods store, and the Browns set up housekeeping in a small, two-room log cabin near the mine where J.J. worked. Before long, Margaret found that she was going to have a baby.

In the summer of 1887, Margaret left Leadville to return to Hannibal for the birth of her first child. Mortality rates were high in those days, for both mother and newborn, and Margaret probably wanted to be in familiar surroundings with her mother and other family members by her side for the event. Lawrence Palmer Brown was born on August 30, 1887, in the same little cottage on Denkler's Alley where his mother had been born just twenty years before. Margaret stayed in Hannibal throughout the winter months, and the Browns' newborn son was baptized by Reverend M.J. McLaughlin at the Church of the Immaculate Conception in Hannibal. As soon as the weather permitted travel the next spring, Margaret and six-month-old Larry boarded the westbound train leaving Union Depot and returned to their Leadville home in the mountains of Colorado.

These were the salad days for J.J. and Margaret; they were young and in love, with their whole future ahead of them. In the fall of 1888, the Browns moved into a larger Leadville home at 322 West Seventh Street just a few blocks from Daniel and the Landrigans that featured a formal parlor, several bedrooms, a separate kitchen and high ceilings. The next spring, John and Johanna Tobin sold their home on Denkler's Alley for $700 and joined their children in Leadville, bringing with them William, aged nineteen, and Helen, who was now nearly eighteen. John Tobin, who was now in his sixties, was named the watchman at the mine that J.J. supervised. Just before little Larry's second birthday, J.J. and Margaret welcomed a daughter, Catherine Ellen, whom they called Helen, who was born in Leadville on July 1, 1889.

Both J.J. and Margaret continued their education, with Margaret studying reading and literature with a private tutor and taking music lessons from Mrs. Wooster in Leadville. As J.J.'s stature in the community grew, Margaret wanted to present herself as his equal partner and earn a corresponding amount of respect in the community; displaying the strong social conscience that she had developed as a young girl in Hannibal, Margaret began to offer her time with civic organizations working for the betterment of the

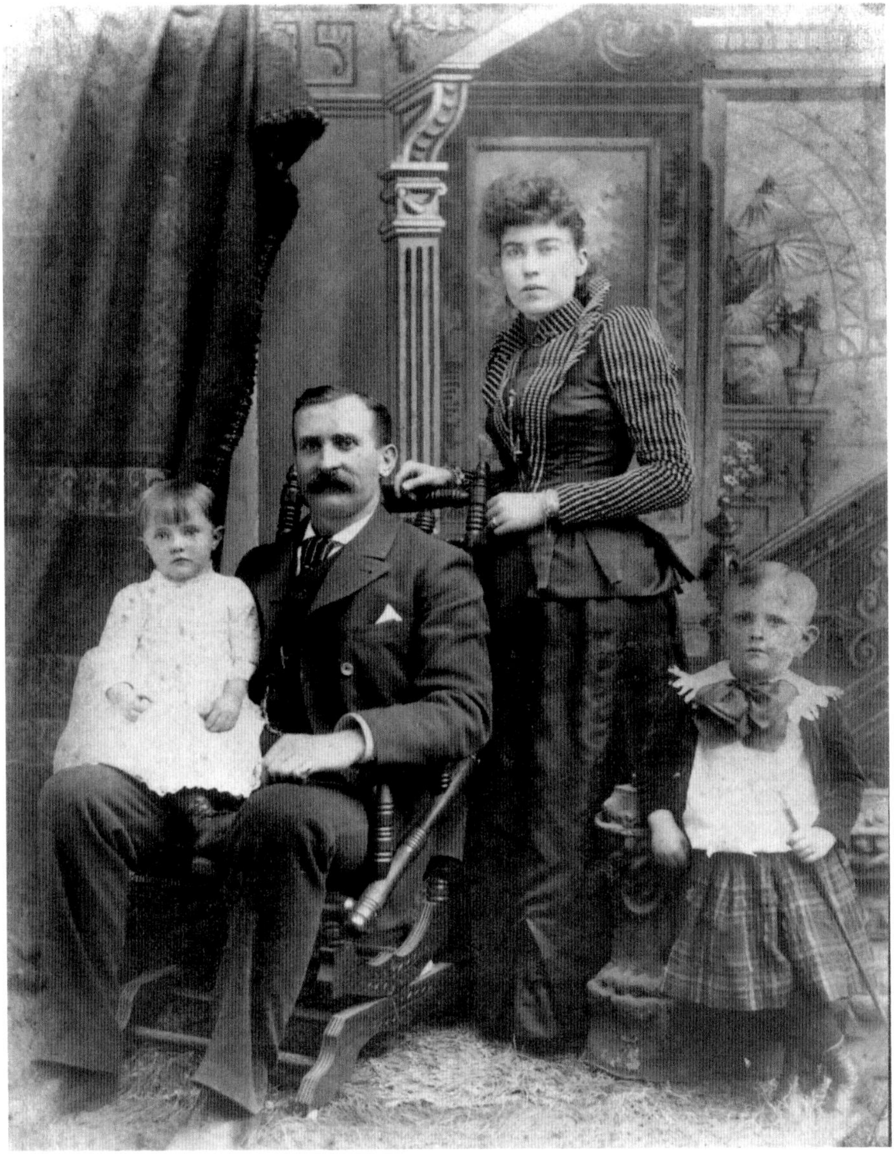

The Brown family portrait taken in Leadville, circa 1890. *From left to right*: Helen, J.J., Margaret and Lawrence. *Courtesy of History Colorado, 10025274.*

community, particularly in the education of Leadville's immigrant women and children. Margaret was also on hand for the formation of the Colorado chapter of the American Woman Suffrage Association, which set up its offices in the Tabor Opera House building on Harrison Avenue.

Because of J.J.'s leadership position at the mines, the Browns, who were not wealthy, would still have been considered a bit higher in class than those who labored in the mines. But down-to-earth Margaret never let this go to her head and was always found to be warm and gracious. "I can remember often taking packages from the store to their home," recalled Thomas Cahill many years later in a letter written to Lawrence Brown, "and your Mother always asked me to come in, sit down, and have a piece of her homemade cake or pie. You can easily imagine what a hit that would make with a little boy. I was so impressed with her kindness and thoughtfulness that the memory of her has remained with me always."

The Luck of the Irish

In 1893, an event occurred that would change J.J. and Margaret Brown's lives forever. The silver mines in Leadville were successful thanks in large part to the Sherman Silver Purchase Act of 1890, which required the U.S. government to purchase as much as 4.5 million ounces of silver bullion each month, thereby artificially increasing the demand for silver. The government would issue Treasury Notes with which to purchase the silver that could be redeemed for either silver or gold. As silver production increased, however, the price of silver began to decrease; most investors redeemed their notes for the higher-priced gold, which soon depleted the government's gold reserves. After the Panic of 1893 commenced, newly elected president Grover Cleveland oversaw the repeal of the Sherman Act, forcing the government to purchase gold to increase the government's gold supplies. The price of silver began to plummet overnight.

Leadville felt the effects immediately. Within a matter of days, the mines were forced to cease their operations, some laying off their entire workforces. Banks and downtown businesses closed. At one point in the summer of 1893, Leadville reached unemployment levels of 90 percent. The town of Leadville was devastated, and Margaret and other members of the Brown and Tobin families went to work assisting the unemployed, setting up soup kitchens and arranging temporary shelters for those in need.

Earlier that year, J.J. had been appointed superintendent of all properties owned by the Ibex Mining Company in Leadville. Ibex owned a number of shafts in the area, including Shaft No. 1, the Little Jonny Mine. This

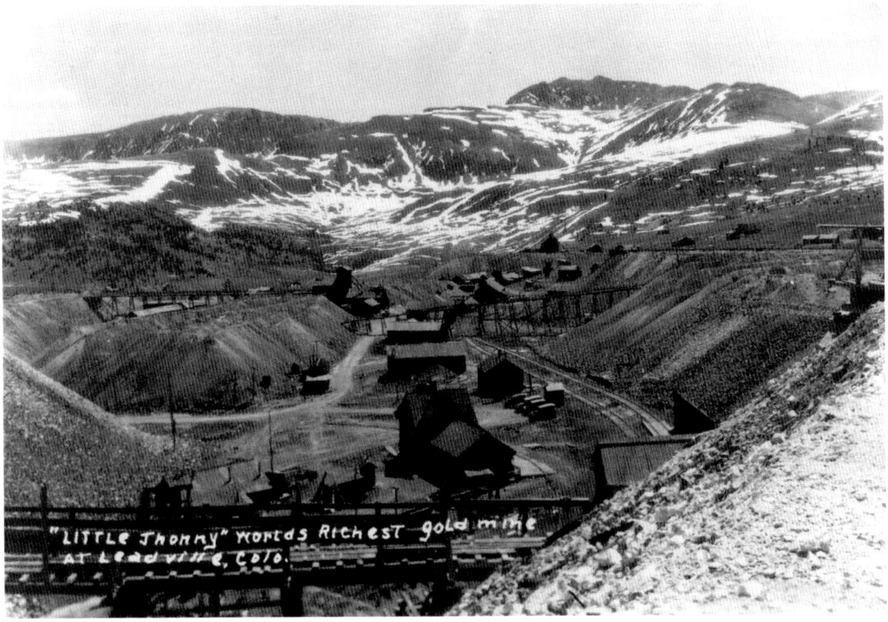

J.J. Brown's engineering savvy led to one of the biggest gold discoveries in Colorado's history at the Little Jonny Mine in 1893. *Courtesy of History Colorado, 10025272.*

particular mine had remained elusive for quite some time, as the shaft contained too much dolomite sand to make it safe for miners to enter without fear of collapse. Although Leadville had plunged into a deep recession with the repeal of the Sherman Act, the board of directors at Ibex decided to continue to invest in Leadville and pursue new revenue streams, and the board encouraged Superintendent Brown to find a way to shore up the walls of the shaft so that they could finally mine Little Jonny.

Using nothing more than timbers and bales of hay to hold back the sand, J.J. was able to secure the shaft and send miners into Little Jonny. Once inside, they struck an enormous vein of gold and copper. It was a monumental achievement, one that would turn around fortunes in Leadville for many years to come. On October 29, 1893, the *Leadville Herald Democrat* proclaimed, "The Little Jonnie [*sic*] is shipping 135 tons of good ore per day."

The Ibex Mining Company was able to pay its shareholders $1 million in dividends in the next year. To recognize his contribution to the company, they rewarded J.J. with 12,500 shares of Ibex stock and a seat on the board of directors. J.J. Brown was now a very wealthy man.

To celebrate, J.J. took his family on an extended vacation. They traveled across the United States for months, visiting family and friends and making a stop in Hannibal. They visited the Columbian Exposition, the 1893 World's Fair in Chicago, where Margaret marveled at the exotic peoples from all around the world and the amazing exhibits that celebrated faraway lands that most Americans, including Margaret at the time, could only dream of visiting.

The Denver Browns

Although their fortunes were made there, few of the mine owners lived in Leadville; most of the grand homes of wealthy Coloradoans were found in Denver. In April 1894, the Browns decided to relocate and become Denverites, and soon J.J. and Margaret had purchased a beautiful home located at 1340 Pennsylvania Avenue in the fashionable, upper-class Capitol Hill district, just a few blocks from the state capitol. The home had been built five years earlier for Isaac and Mary Large; Isaac had made his fortune in silver mining, but after the repeal of the Sherman Act, he had lost a good deal of his fortune and was unable to keep the home.

The house was designed by architect William Lang. Featuring elements of Queen Anne, Richardsonian Romanesque and Neoclassic elements, the stone façade includes both rough rhyolite stone and smooth red sandstone. Inside, exquisite woodwork adorns the large entry foyer and is carried throughout the first floor in the formal parlor, library and dining room. Upstairs houses seven rooms on the second floor, including an indoor bath, and servant's quarters on the third floor. For its time, the home featured all modern conveniences, including four fireplaces, electricity, the latest in indoor plumbing, radiated steam heat and a new hand-crank telephone. Because of the two stone lions that guarded the front entry, the house was nicknamed the "House of Lions." The size, scope, décor and style of the House of Lions is reminiscent of the homes of the lumber barons one would have found during the same time period on Hannibal's Millionaires' Row.

Over the next several years, the Brown family was very busy. J.J., still working with Ibex but now also purchasing mines of his own and investing heavily throughout the western states, was frequently called out of town on business. Daniel Tobin, Margaret's elder brother, took over as

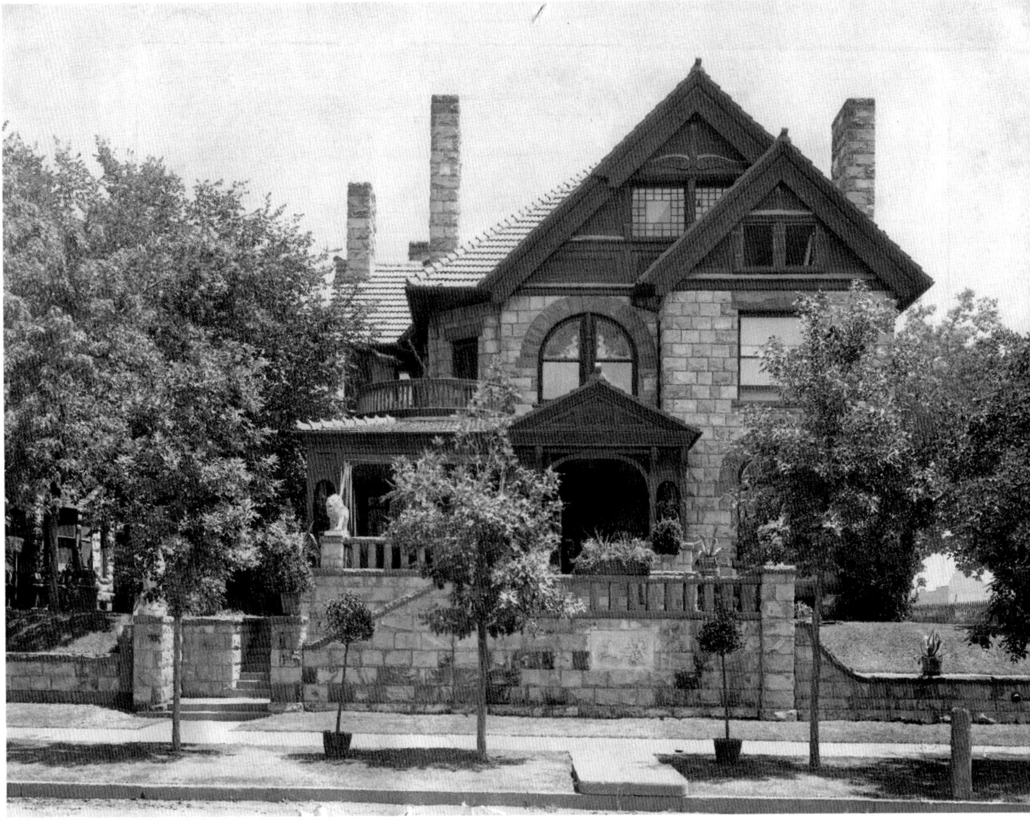

The House of Lions on Pennsylvania Avenue in Denver was a primary residence for the Brown family until 1909, when J.J. gave the house to Margaret as one of the conditions in their legal separation. *Courtesy of Molly Brown House Museum.*

manager of J.J.'s various business dealings in Leadville. Other members of the Brown and Tobin families would also join J.J.'s staff of employees, and any relation interested in learning mining was welcome to become a part of the family business.

While Lawrence and Helen were in school and J.J. was away traveling for business, Margaret kept herself busy. She began to make her way into Denver's social circles, volunteering her time and money to various charitable causes. Although Margaret knew that these organizations were working to raise money and awareness to help combat real problems in their community, and took these efforts very seriously, she was also well aware of what was expected of "women of means"—luncheons, charity events, benefits, theater openings and dinner parties—and was eager to attend these exciting social gatherings. Although she'd had a taste of "society" in Leadville, and was certainly considered a leader in that community, Denver was quite a different story. Margaret was curious about the opportunities her newfound wealth would provide her in Denver, and Denver was equally curious about the *nouveau riche* Mrs. J.J. Brown.

The *Denver Times* reported on Margaret Brown's introduction to society:

> *Social annals record that when Mrs. Brown first made her bow to Denver society it was under the friendly chaperonage of Mrs. J.B. Grant. When the wife of the millionaire mine owner first came to the city it was the Grants who were the first to welcome her. It was in their box at the theater that she was the observed of all observers. It was the Grants' carriage that might be seen at any day and hour waiting before the Brown residence while the owner visited with the witty young matron from the mountains who had yet to make her way into Denver society.*

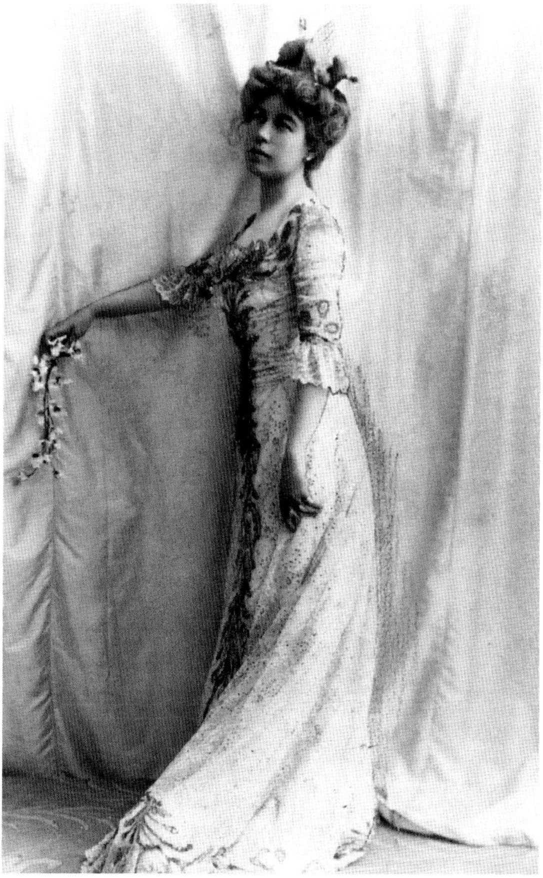

An early portrait of Margaret in society dress. *Courtesy of History Colorado, 10029154.*

Mary Matteson Grant was the wife of Colorado's third governor, James Benton Grant (governor from 1883 to 1885). Grant, who had extensive training in mining, had migrated to Leadville in the early 1880s and formed the Omaha and Grant Smelting Company with his uncle in 1882. The Grants had befriended J.J. Brown while they lived in Leadville and were pleased to assist in introducing the Browns when J.J. and Margaret moved to Denver ten years later.

Margaret found early on that society life suited her. She enjoyed entertaining and decorated their home in the lavish style popular during the Gilded Age. To overcome the stigma that *nouveau riche* somehow translated into "lack of style," Margaret studied fashion and was adept at setting just the right tone with her gowns and accessories. The society columns quickly took note and began to regularly report on the fashionable Mrs. Brown. After a luncheon party Margaret hosted at the House of Lions, the *Denver Times* gave its stamp of approval, reporting that "the appointments of the entire affair were perfect to the minutest detail."

The Vale of Avoca

The Browns made their first voyage across the sea in early 1895. Lawrence, now eight, and Helen, six, accompanied J.J. and Margaret and set sail from New York, arriving in Naples, Italy, on April 10, 1895. After spending several months in Italy, they enjoyed an extended tour of England, Scotland and Ireland. While on the Emerald Isle, it is likely that Margaret would have wanted to visit Fermoy to see the place of her father's birth. This journey had a profound effect on Margaret—to see the world and to learn of new places, new languages and new customs became some of the biggest passions of her life. For Margaret, this was just the first of many travels across the North Atlantic.

To escape the pollution and noise of the busy city, J.J. decided to purchase property near Bear Creek, just nine miles outside Denver. He and Margaret wanted to build a country estate of their own, a place where the children could ride horses and roam freely, as well as a place where they could entertain guests. In 1895, J.J. purchased a total of four hundred acres and commenced construction of their summer home. The foursquare-style Victorian, built according to J.J. and Margaret's wishes, was practical and inviting rather than ostentatious. It stood near the midway point of a tall hill and was constructed of red "buttered" brick, with long, wide porches surrounding two sides. Behind the house, the large brick barn was equipped with a hardwood floor for dancing parties. The front lawns were manicured with a circular drive and fountain; a fully stocked fishing pond was also on the property. Here J.J. dreamed of raising thoroughbred horses, planting crops and harvesting vast orchards.

Margaret chose to name the estate Avoca after one of her favorite poems, "The Meeting of the Waters," written by the Irish poet Thomas Moore. Inspired by a visit with friends to the Vale of Avoca (in County Wicklow, Ireland), Moore wrote the poem as a lyric to an old Irish tune, "The Old Head of Dennis." The last verse is written:

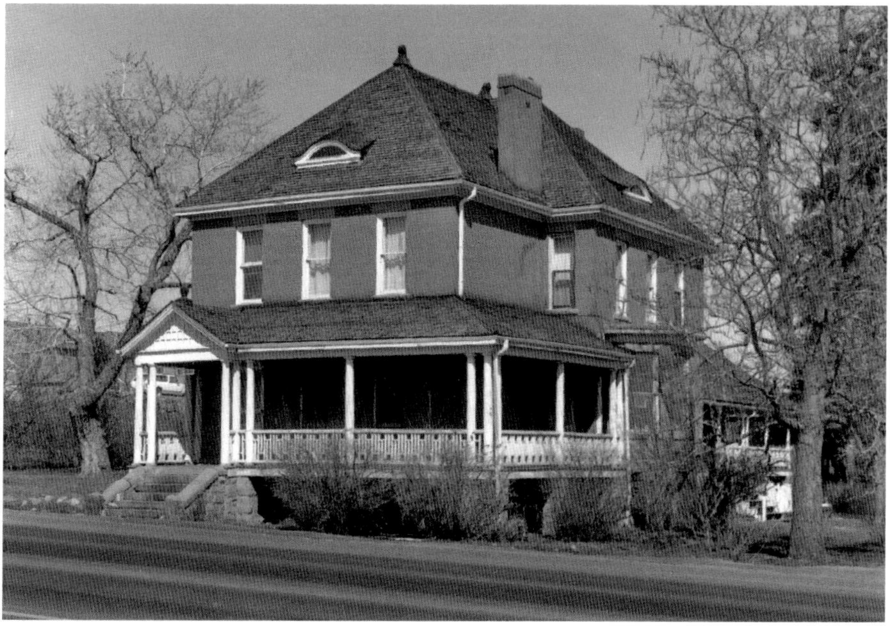

Avoca served as a country home for the Brown family from 1895 to 1910. *Courtesy of the Molly Brown Summer House Museum.*

Sweet vale of Avoca! How calm could I rest
In thy sweet bosom of shade with the friends I love best
Where the storms that we feel in this cold world should cease
And our hearts, like thy waters, be mingled in peace,
And our hearts, like thy waters, be mingled in peace.

J.J. enjoyed tinkering with his farm, and even though it was intended to be a source of recreation, his entrepreneurial spirit could not help but see potential profits from his rural endeavors. He constructed a two-story chicken house where ten thousand specialty hens were raised and sold to posh Denver restaurants. These pampered fowl were treated to a specialty diet, custom-built heated incubators, their own hospital and a yard for exercise and sunshine. Near the "coop," another structure was built so that specialty pigeons could also be raised and sold to fine dining establishments. One hundred acres of hay were planted, and jams and jellies were made from more than one thousand fruit trees in the orchards of Avoca. Caretakers were instructed to send the bounty from Avoca's harvests to the Browns' Denver home for their enjoyment in the winter months.

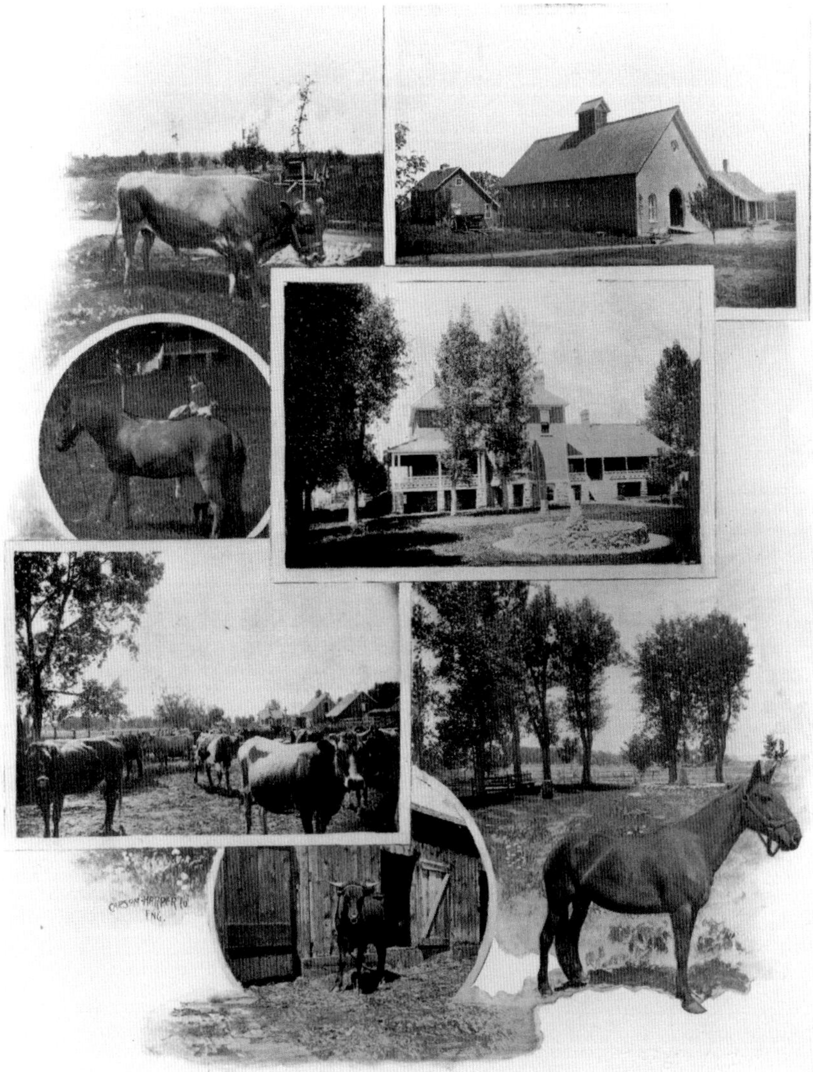

TYPICAL SCENES AT AVOCA LODGE—J. J. BROWN'S RANCH, NEAR DENVER.

Scenes of the Brown family's country estate, Avoca, circa 1905. *Courtesy of Denver Public Library.*

Summers at Avoca were happy times for the Brown family. Guests to Avoca arrived by carriage or train, not only from Denver and Leadville but also from Hannibal, Chicago and New York, and some would stay for weeks at a time. Grand parties were held, with music and dancing in the barn. Day trips into the surrounding foothills included hunting, fishing and picnicking, with views of the mighty Rocky Mountains in the near distance. Lawrence and Helen enjoyed their adventures on the farm as well and spent many fun-filled hours driving their pony cart around the property. Avoca may have been the place where the Brown family remembered being the happiest after their move to Denver.

The Browns never ceased giving the newspapers fodder for the society columns. The Denver newspapers kept track of the Browns' comings and goings, regularly reporting on the visitors they entertained at Avoca, as well as their own travels abroad. Guests clamored for an invitation to relax with the Browns in the quiet splendor of Avoca, and their events at the summer estate were the talk of the town. As Kristen Iversen explained in her biography of Margaret, "From 1894 to the early 1920s, the Browns took up more space in Denver's society pages than nearly any other Denver family and were regularly listed on the Social Register. Margaret and J.J. were not ostracized by Denver society—they *were* Denver society."

Unfortunately, throughout these years, while the society columns were reporting on Margaret's wardrobe and dinner parties, they also reported on rumors that had begun to circulate about J.J. Brown. With extended absences from home required so that J.J. could tend to his business dealings, suspicions of unfaithfulness began to surface. "J.J.'s life in Leadville was always full of gossip," one paper reported, "as he had a reputation for being a ladies man and was extremely popular." It seems that the charming, irresistible Mr. Brown whom Margaret fell in love with back in Leadville was indeed charming and irresistible.

To keep her mind off any unfortunate rumors, and as the money continued to roll in, Margaret became more and more involved with her civic organizations and philanthropic pursuits. She became a charter member of the Denver Women's Club and also the Denver Women's Press Club, which had specific guidelines for its members: "No woman shall be admitted to the club who is a bore; who holds out on newspaper reporters; who has not a proper respect for the power of the press; and who cannot do something to drive dull cares away." She and J.J. joined the Denver Country Club, and each season they purchased their own box at the Broadway Theater, where Margaret delighted in attending plays and operas just as she had as a young lady at the Park Theater in Hannibal and the Tabor Opera House in Leadville.

For a time, Lawrence and Helen attended Sacred Heart College, a parochial school in Denver, but eventually they were both enrolled in studies

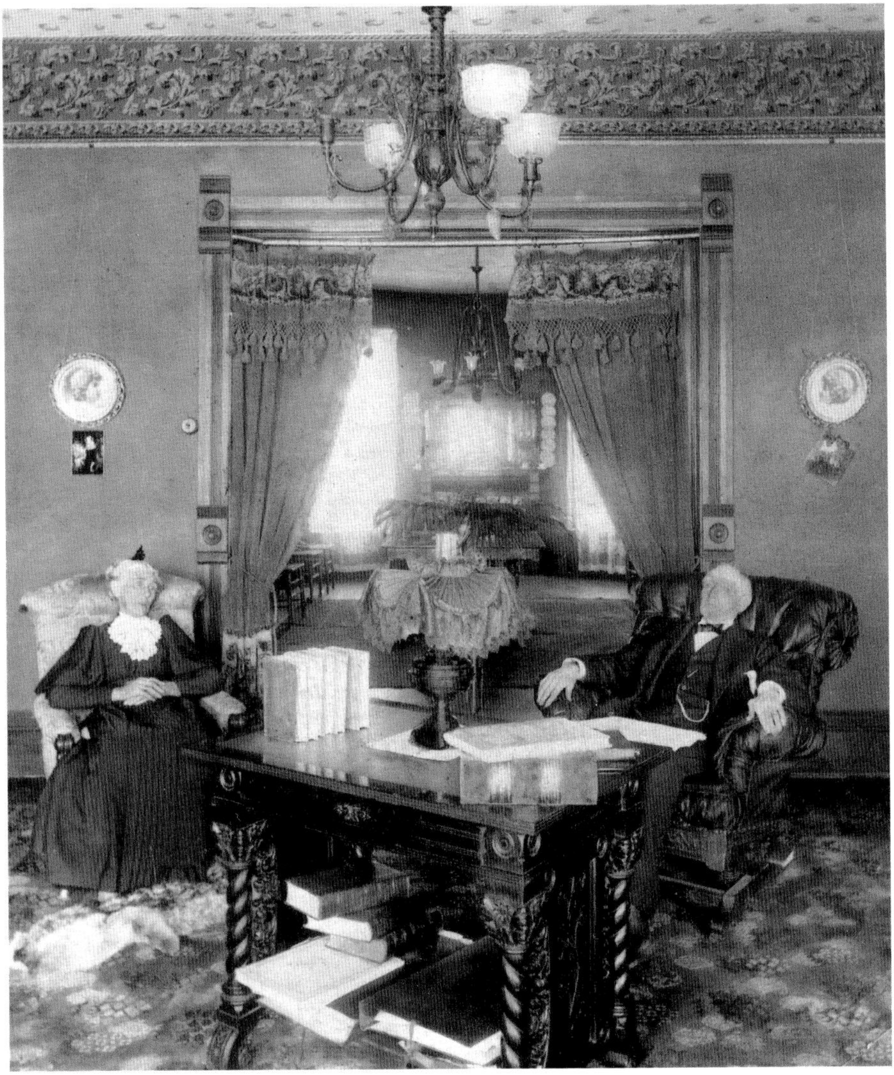

John and Johanna Tobin reclining in the library room at the House of Lions. *Courtesy of History Colorado, 10025276.*

in France—Helen at the Convent of Notre Dame in Paris and Lawrence at Jean D'Arc College. It was the realization of a dream for Margaret that her children be educated at the finest Catholic institutions in Europe, and she was delighted when they were accepted.

In the spring of 1899, Margaret was to return to her hometown of Hannibal on a somber note. Her beloved father, John Tobin, had died at the age of seventy-six. He and Johanna were living at the House of Lions where he died of heart disease on April 20. His passing was a sad episode for all of the Browns; J.J. recalled many long conversations in his study with John, smoking cigars and discussing the latest news in politics and baseball. "Grandfather Tobin was the favorite of all," James Benziger later wrote. "My mother [Helen], a great reader from childhood, spent much of her time in a rocking chair in his room." Margaret, her mother and her brothers and sisters accompanied their father's body to Hannibal, where he was buried at St. Mary's Cemetery. Johanna would follow her husband in death six years later and would be laid to rest beside him in Hannibal. Although their passing was devastating for Margaret, she could be proud of the fact that she and J.J. had pulled John and Johanna Tobin out of poverty and given them a comfortable life in their twilight years. They had enjoyed living their final days at Avoca and in the House of Lions with their children and grandchildren around them. Margaret had made them proud and very, very happy.

The Dawn of a New Century

At the turn of the new century, Americans across the country had a renewed sense of optimism, eagerly anticipating all that the twentieth century would bring. Margaret, too, began to look ahead to her next challenge. Perhaps she sensed that she was outgrowing Denver or realized that her ambition was greater than the opportunities that Denver could offer her; either way, Margaret began to look beyond the horizon.

With Helen overseas in France at school, and Lawrence enrolled in St. John's College in Fordham, New York, Margaret made a bold move and decided to attend college. In an era that deemed adult education a privilege only afforded to a chosen few (who were usually male), the Carnegie Institute, financed by steel magnate Andrew Carnegie, made higher education available to anyone who wished to further themselves regardless of race, gender or socioeconomic status. Margaret was one of the institute's first enrollees. While attending Carnegie, located in Pittsburgh, Pennsylvania, Margaret studied literature, language and dramatic arts, traveling back home between semesters.

When she arrived back in Denver for the Christmas holiday in 1901, she was met with shocking news: J.J. was being sued for $50,000 by Harry D.

Call of Colorado for alienation of his wife's affection. Maude Morton Call, reported to be a "tall blonde with a splendid figure," had met J.J. Brown at a resort in Pueblo and, shortly thereafter, left behind her husband and three-year-old son to be with him. The press had a field day with the news. Margaret would have to deal with the scandal and would not return to her studies at Carnegie. J.J. ended the adulterous relationship and settled the lawsuit with Mr. Call out of court.

In an effort to repair the damage done to their marriage, and to escape the spotlight of the press in Denver, J.J. and Margaret decided to travel. They turned Avoca over to tenants and announced that they would spend the next several years in Ireland. This trip only lasted about a year, however, and afterward the couple returned to the House of Lions. Soon, they were again traveling abroad. In 1902, J.J. secured a special passport, and the couple, with a servant in tow, spent a great amount of time in Asia, visiting Yokohama and Tokyo in Japan, Shanghai and Hong Kong in China and Bombay and Calcutta in India. Margaret would write a travelogue for the *Denver Republican* upon her return, making clear her disapproval toward the English for allowing the citizens of India's most populated urban areas to live in such abject poverty.

After these extended trips abroad, J.J. resumed the management of his various business enterprises, and Margaret rolled up her sleeves and got back to her charitable works. In 1903, she joined forces with Judge Ben Lindsey and championed the juvenile justice system he advocated, hosting fundraisers both in Denver and at Avoca.

In that same year, the Countess Leary came to Denver and stayed with Margaret for several weeks. Annie Leary was the daughter of a wealthy New York milliner, and due to her philanthropic efforts related to her Catholic faith, Pope Leo XIII had conferred on Annie the title of "Countess of the Holy See." Archbishop Corrigan of New York named a chapel in her honor, as well. In return for Margaret's graciousness in Denver, Countess Leary entertained Margaret and Helen in her homes on Fifth Avenue in New York and in Newport, Rhode Island. The countess was delighted to introduce Margaret into Newport society where Margaret would soon become acquainted with the Astors and Vanderbilts.

When the urge to travel struck, Margaret, usually with daughter Helen along for the ride (but without J.J.), would set sail for an overseas adventure, always stopping in Paris at some point along the way regardless of which country was the feature on the trip's itinerary. The Browns spent the summer of 1904 enjoying the St. Louis World's Fair, traveling several times by train between St. Louis and nearby Hannibal to enjoy the festivities.

As her prowess for fundraising became well known, Margaret was approached by the young Denver priest Hugh L. McMenamin, called Father Mac, who wished to see a great cathedral built in Denver. The property for the cathedral, eight lots at the corner of East Colfax Avenue and Logan Street, located less than three blocks from the House of Lions, had been purchased by J.J. Brown, John Campion, John K. Mullen and Dennis Sheedy several years before but construction had been delayed due to lack of funding. Margaret was happy to oblige Father Mac's request, and the two began to work on a grand event to raise the necessary funds to begin construction of the cathedral.

Margaret proposed a festival she called "The Carnival of Nations." No doubt this was inspired by her experiences at Chicago's Columbia Exposition in 1893 and the St. Louis World's Fair in 1904. The Carnival of Nations would be a living history exhibit, with nations from all over the world represented by a "village" that presented their particular culture with authentically costumed attendants. Different booths were spotlighted on different nights; Margaret took particular interest in the booth representing Ireland, holding an Irish dance at the dancing pavilion, with instructors on hand to assist those not adept in the art of clogging. The carnival covered five acres near the corner of Colfax and Broadway, and at 8:30 p.m. on opening night, July 10, 1906, Colorado governor Jesse McDonald oversaw the illumination of ten thousand specially placed lights donated by the Denver Gas & Electric Company.

The Carnival of Nations ran for sixteen days and, although cut short due to the limited availability of the property, was deemed a great success. Nearly $15,000 was raised, and on July 15, 1906, the cornerstone of the cathedral was laid. Six years later, a crowd of more than twenty thousand Denverites would be on hand to witness the dedication of the Immaculate Conception Cathedral on October 27, 1912, where ten thousand parishioners knelt outside near the front steps to receive the benediction of the blessed sacrament. This landmark structure still serves the Catholics of Denver today, now known as the Cathedral Basilica of the Immaculate Conception.

Throughout the ensuing years, J.J. and Margaret continued to grow apart. Her life was a whirlwind of social engagements, fundraising and travel. J.J.

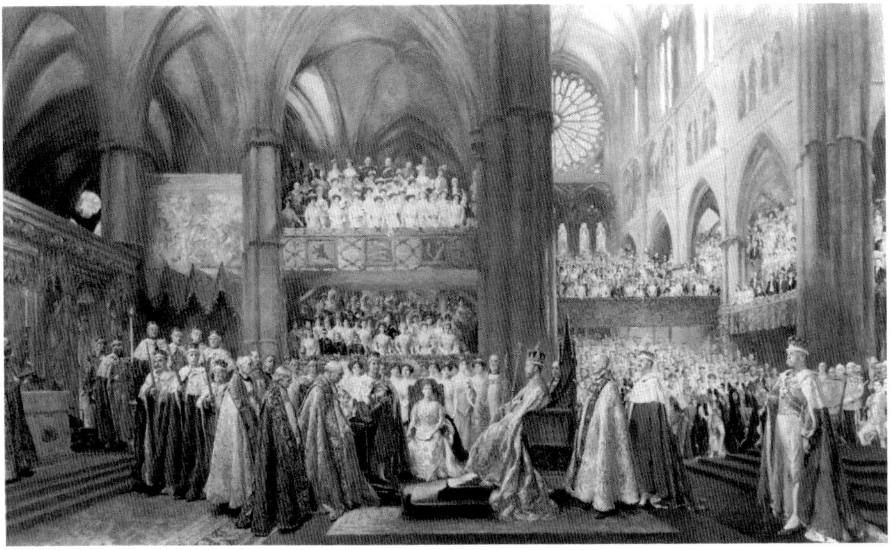

Margaret knew that she had reached the heights of high society when she and her daughter, Helen, were invited to the coronation of King George V at Westminster Abbey. *Courtesy of the Library of Congress.*

became more and more anchored to the West and kept busy with his various business dealings. Lawrence and Helen attended school, withdrew for the chance to take an extended trip with their mother and enrolled in a new school afterward. After enjoying summers in Avoca for ten years, the house was eventually rented and the grounds sold off in parcels. When J.J. and Margaret agreed to legally separate in 1909, the House of Lions was also let to renters; on occasions when Margaret would return to Denver, she would take rooms at the Brown Palace Hotel.

Margaret's meteoric rise through society circles had no bounds. In 1911, Margaret and Helen attended the coronation of King George V in Westminster Abbey, just after Helen had been presented at the drawing room of the English Court in May of that year.

Lawrence and Eileen married in 1911 while Margaret was visiting Europe with Helen. That autumn, as John Jacob Astor IV and his young bride, Madeline, were celebrating their honeymoon by visiting the Great Pyramids of Egypt with Margaret and Helen Brown, Lawrence and Eileen were blessed with their first child, Lawrence Jr., who was born on November 21, 1911. Five months later, when the baby seemed to be getting along poorly, Lawrence sent a telegram to his mother at the Ritz Hotel in Paris, asking her to return to Missouri as quickly as possible to help care for the child.

Part VII

Culture Knows No Boundaries

When J.J. Brown died, he left no will. Or, at least, none that could be found. Margaret knew that this was highly unusual as J.J. was a shrewd businessman and kept meticulous records, but her children, particularly Helen and her husband, George, insisted that there was no will. As J.J.'s legal wife, Margaret requested that the court name her as administrator of the estate, but the court denied her request. Margaret's legal team began to find discrepancies in the estate's bookkeeping and were alarmed to realize that, shortly before his death, a large transfer of assets had occurred from J.J. to the children, and these funds were not being included as part of J.J.'s final estate.

Helen insisted that the funds she'd received were given to her by her father to fulfill J.J.'s promise to buy each of his children a home. Lawrence had been given a house purchased by his father in LaJolla, California, where Lawrence was currently in residence. Yet at the time of the transfer of funds, Helen had not been able to find a house which suited her, and she claimed that J.J. had given her the money so that it would be available when she found what she was looking for.

Margaret grew suspicious, however, when on July 3, 1925, the *Denver Post* reported that $207,686.38 had been transferred to Helen and Lawrence before J.J.'s death, far more money than Helen would have required to purchase a suitable home. One possible explanation that came to light that seemed more plausible was that just prior to the transfer, J.J. had received notice that he was being sued once again for an alleged affair,

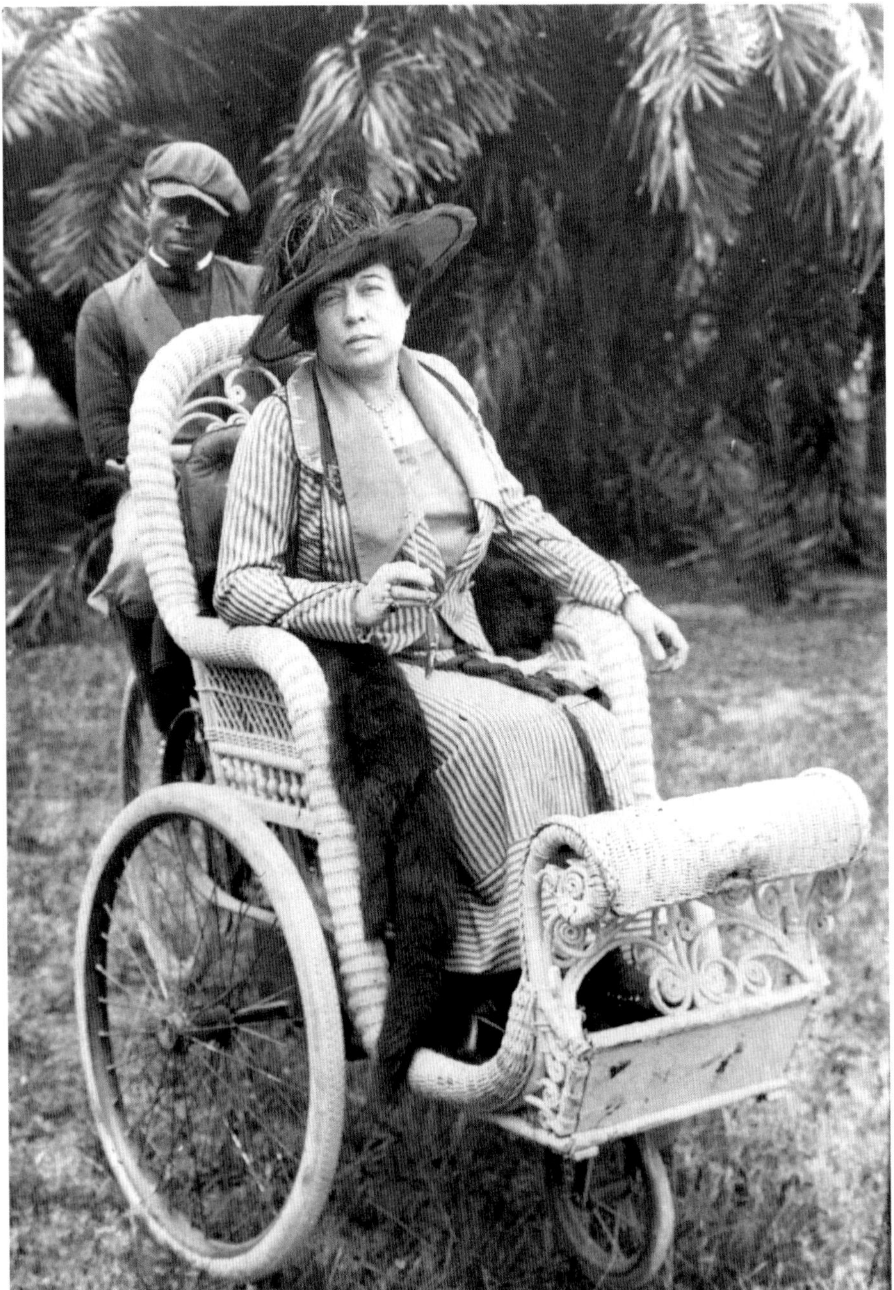

Margaret Tobin Brown vacationing in Palm Beach, Florida, late 1920s. *Courtesy of History Colorado, 10026079.*

this time with a woman named Sabra Simpson. J.J. must have feared an unfavorable outcome if this case had gone to court and may have transferred the funds into his children's names to protect the money. J.J. was eventually able to settle the case out of court, but the funds were never transferred back to his estate.

Tensions worsened between Margaret and her children. Both sides were distrustful, suspicious that the other was withholding information from the court. Margaret's children accused her of mental instability and argued that if she were given a cash settlement, she would not be able to properly manage the funds, squandering them on extravagance.

During the legal wrangling, Margaret began to have difficulty meeting her financial obligations. She was forced to withdraw from her home in Newport, and although she still owned the House of Lions, Margaret spent many years living in hotels between Denver, Hannibal, Newport, Paris and Palm Beach, Florida.

Finally, in 1926, against Margaret's objections and without her official signature, Judge George A. Luxford approved the final settlement: Margaret would receive $100,000 in trust that was not to be accessible to her, but she would be granted use of the interest and dividends for her personal expenses. Helen and Lawrence would also be awarded $100,000 and would not have to return any of the funds transferred to them by their father just prior to his death.

Although Helen had technically "won" the legal battle, after the settlement, she spurned her mother because of disparaging statements Margaret had made against her husband, George Benziger, during the hearings. Margaret, out of anger, removed Helen and Lawrence from her will. The rift between them would remain for several years.

Eventually, Margaret would reconcile with Helen and Lawrence, although Margaret would never find herself to be as close to them as she once was. With Lawrence in California and Helen in New York, Margaret would increasingly spend time traveling to and fro, particularly overseas with her European friends.

Submerged with Cheers

Margaret returned to Hannibal frequently, often staying with her elder sister Katie and her husband, John Becker, who lived at 322 North

Street, a short distance from Denkler's Alley. On May 27, 1926, Margaret was visiting Hannibal to attend the dedication of a special statue to honor Mark Twain. Commissioned by George A. Mahan, the bronze statue was the first in the United States depicting fictional characters, Tom Sawyer and Huckleberry Finn. Mahan, who had the foresight to purchase Mark Twain's boyhood home in 1911 shortly after Twain's death to preserve it in his honor, had also commissioned from sculptor Frederick C. Hibbard the statue of Twain overlooking the Mississippi River in Riverview Park. As president of the Missouri State Historical Society, Mahan was instrumental in the historic preservation of many of the sites in Hannibal associated with Mark Twain, sites that have since been visited by millions of guests making the pilgrimage to Mark Twain's beloved boyhood hometown. The Tom and Huck statue was placed at the foot of Cardiff Hill, where it remains today.

While attending the statue's dedication, Margaret encouraged Clara Gabrilowitsch, Mark Twain's daughter, to donate many of Twain's personal belongings to the Mark Twain Home Foundation in Hannibal. These treasured artifacts are still on display and are the cornerstone of exhibits at the Mark Twain Museum Gallery, along with sketches and original paintings by Norman Rockwell commissioned for special editions of *The Adventures of Tom Sawyer* and *Adventures of Huckleberry Finn* in the 1930s.

Inspired by the efforts of George Mahan to preserve Twain's legacy in Hannibal, another historic preservation project was spearheaded during this time by Margaret back in Denver. Eugene Field, the American writer best known for his children's poetry and humorous essays, was a fellow Missouri native who, born in St. Louis, had lived in Denver from 1881 to 1883 in the Washington Park neighborhood. Margaret purchased the Eugene Field cottage and had it moved to the edge of Washington Park, financing the relocation and restoration herself. For many years, the Eugene Field House was used as a branch of the Denver Public Library and is still open to the public today. The house was listed on the National Register of Historic Places in 1979.

At the age of sixty, Margaret was able to pursue yet another goal she had dreamed of throughout her life: becoming a renowned stage actress. Since childhood, Margaret had been enamored of the theater, charmed by actors,

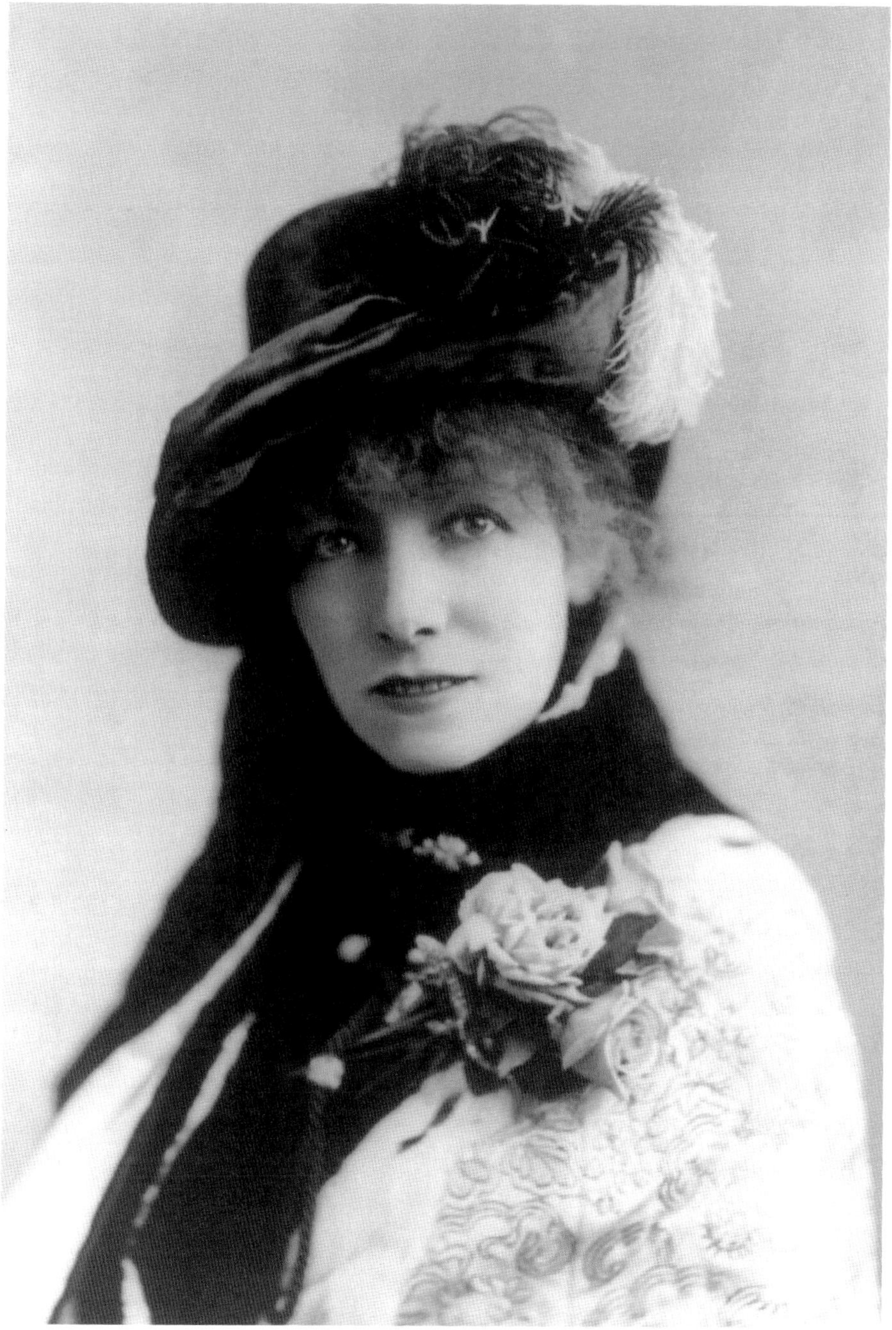

The famed French actress Sarah Bernhardt. Margaret appeared on stage reprising Bernhardt's most famous role in *L'Aiglon*. *Courtesy of the Library of Congress.*

singers and musicians and always finding the greatest pleasure in their company. In the second half of the 1920s, Margaret traveled to Paris and began studies under a former instructor of her idol, the legendary French stage and film star Sarah Bernhardt. Soon, Margaret was on stage performing in productions of *The Merchant of Venice* and *Cleopatra*. Her ambition, however, was to reprise the role made famous by Bernhardt: Napoleon II of France, Duke of Reichstadt, in the play *L'Aiglon*.

Though some were skeptical that a woman of Margaret's age could play the part of a young man (*L'Aiglon* translates to "Young Eagle"), Margaret seemed undaunted. She explained, "Some people find it strange that an American woman should aspire to play the roles of Bernhardt. I recall, too, that some people smirked when I brought home ancient statuary from Egypt and decorated up a few acres of the Rocky Mountains for my home, but I am sure that those who know the place will agree that culture knows no boundaries and that fine arts are international."

Paris newspapers would celebrate Margaret's talents and applaud her performances, reporting that Margaret received international recognition for her success with Bernhardt's roles. In May 1929, she was awarded the Palm of the Academy of France for her interpretations of the works of Sarah Bernhardt and her support of the dramatic arts. In the *Denver Post*, Margaret acknowledged the significance of the award, saying, "Paris is known to be a garden of culture and it takes a lot of assurance, with ability, to be welcomed here. If their rising up and submerging me with cheers is any criterion, I have passed muster."

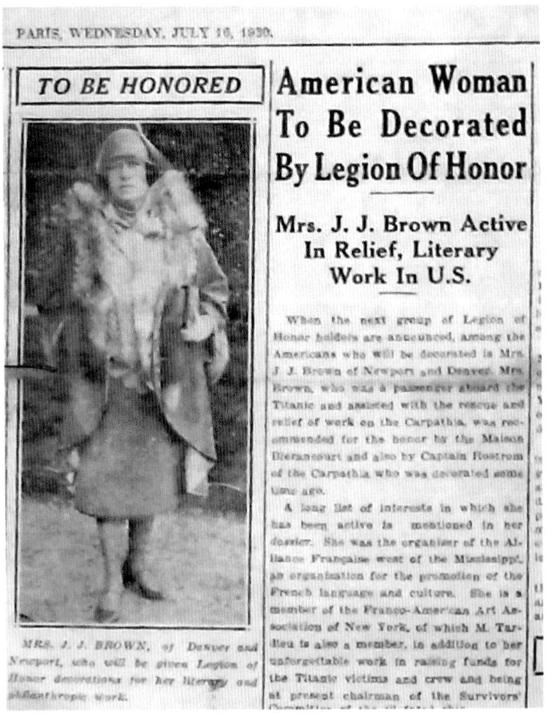

PARIS, WEDNESDAY, JULY 16, 1930.

TO BE HONORED

American Woman To Be Decorated By Legion Of Honor

Mrs. J. J. Brown Active In Relief, Literary Work In U.S.

When the next group of Legion of Honor holders are announced, among the Americans who will be decorated is Mrs. J. J. Brown of Newport and Denver. Mrs. Brown, who was a passenger aboard the Titanic and assisted with the rescue and relief of work on the Carpathia, was recommended for the honor by the Maison Dieramcourt and also by Captain Rostrom of the Carpathia who was decorated some time ago.

A long list of interests in which she has been active is mentioned in her dossier. She was the organiser of the Alliance Française west of the Mississippi, an organisation for the promotion of the French language and culture. She is a member of the Franco-American Art Association of New York, of which M. Tardieu is also a member, in addition to her unforgettable work in raising funds for the Titanic victims and crew and being at present chairman of the Survivors'

MRS. J. J. BROWN, of Denver and Newport, who will be given Legion of Honor decorations for her literary and philanthropic work.

A Paris, France newspaper report on Margaret being awarded the French Legion of Honor medal, 1930. *Author's collection.*

Just three years later, in early 1932, the French

would bestow on Margaret the Legion of Honor medal for her work during the war, as well as other civic and philanthropic contributions she had made on both sides of the Atlantic throughout her life. Captain Rostron, commander of *Carpathia*, had been one of those to nominate Margaret for the honor.

Through the summer of 1932, Margaret would continue to perform *L'Aiglon* at charity events and fundraisers both in Europe and the United States. She took a room at the Barbizon Hotel for Women in New York City at 140 East Sixty-third Street, a popular address for actresses of the time. The impressive twenty-three-story structure, a blend of Italian Renaissance and Late Gothic Revival, was operated as a hotel for women, a safe haven in the world's largest city where no men were allowed above the ground floor and a strict moral and dress code were enforced.

In September 1932, Margaret sent a copy of a brochure from the Barbizon to her housekeeper back at the House of Lions in Denver, Mrs. Edith Stiles, and wrote captions next to the photos in the brochure: "This is my bedroom and my workshop which is piled high to the ceiling with things," "This is my studio on the 19th floor where I practice & I have my friends" and "Here is where the artists I launch give their concerts." Margaret's large, loopy, heavy handwriting nearly covers each page of the document.

On October 26, 1932, at 10:39 p.m., Helen sent a telegram to her brother Lawrence in California:

> *Hempstead NY*
>
> *Lawrence P. Brown*
> *LaJolla, California*
>
> *Mother Died Suddenly Stroke 2pm Presume You Unable Come Funeral Saturday if Agreed*
>
> *Helen*

Margaret had been found in her bed at the Barbizon Hotel. She had died during the night in her sleep from a cerebral hemorrhage. Her funeral

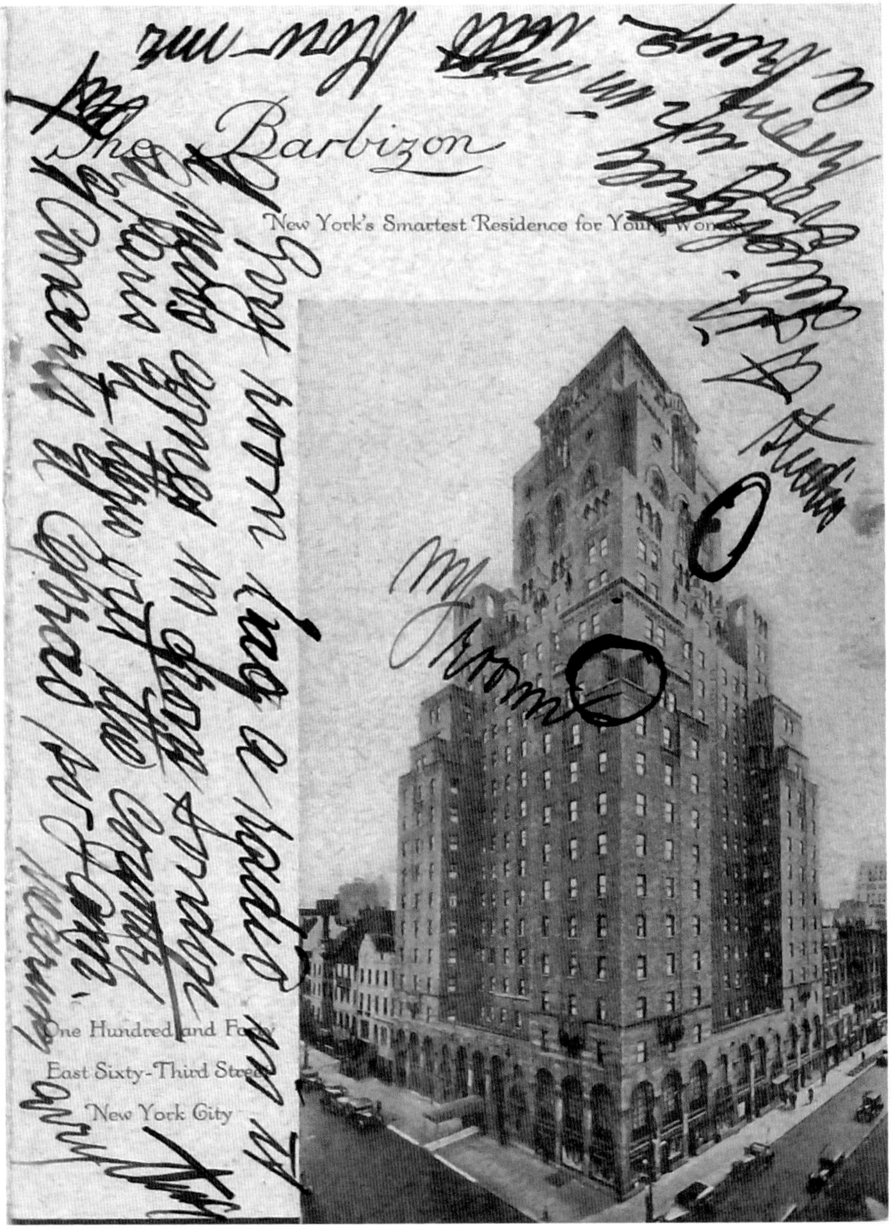

The front cover of a brochure for the Barbizon Hotel for Women in New York City. The brochure was sent to Margaret's housekeeper in Denver, Mrs. Edith Stiles, circa 1932. Margaret wrote on the cover, illustrating where her room was located. *Courtesy of Denver Public Library*.

mass was attended by both of her children, her grandchildren and many of her friends. Helen saw to it that her mother was laid to rest at Holy Rood Cemetery near Helen's home in Long Island, New York, alongside the grave of J.J. Brown. Her personal fortune, valued at approximately $25,000, was distributed according to the wishes of her last will and testament in which she had restored Helen and Lawrence as beneficiaries of her estate.

Margaret left this world exactly as she had wished. As quoted by the *Denver Post* on August 9, 1923, Margaret said:

> *I am a daughter of adventure. This means I never experience a dull moment and must be prepared for any eventuality. I never know when I may go up in an airplane and come down with a crash, or go motoring and climb a pole, or go off for a walk in the twilight and return all mussed up in an ambulance. That's my arc, as the astrologers would say. It's a good one, too, for a person who had rather make a snap-out than a fade-out of life.*

An autopsy was done on the body of Margaret Tobin Brown. The cerebral hemorrhage had been caused by an undiagnosed brain tumor, one that the doctors said had been there for quite some time, possibly as long as the last twenty years of her life. This would date the beginnings of the tumor to coincide with the sinking of *Titanic* in 1912.

Epilogue

Titanic

It was the largest, man-made moving object in the world. The tallest building in Hannibal, rising six stories, was only half its height. The ship would have stretched down Main Street from the Tom and Huck statue at the foot of Cardiff Hill, across Broadway and nearly all the way down South Main Street to Union Depot. It truly was titanic.

Margaret boarded *Titanic* with the Astors and her friend, Emma Bucknell, whose late husband, William Bucknell, was a charter member of the board of trustees and major benefactor of the Pennsylvania university that bore his name. Emma had told Margaret that she was nervous about the trip; it was not unreasonable to be a bit apprehensive about the maiden voyage of a new vessel, but Margaret was comforted to know that Captain Edward Smith, a man whom she knew well and trusted, was at the helm of *Titanic*.

Margaret had done quite a bit of shopping on this trip, collecting the latest European styles of evening and daywear, complete with the shoes, hats, gloves, scarves, jewelry, handbags, shawls and furs that were expected of well-heeled women of the times. Art and sculpture purchased by Margaret on this trip was also being brought back to the States; she was particularly pleased with the acquisition of wonderfully rendered models of Roman ruins that she planned to donate to the Denver Art Museum upon her return. As trunks carrying her wardrobe were being taken to her stateroom, and the three wooden crates containing the art treasures were being loaded into the cargo hold of the great ship, Margaret walked up the gangway and stepped into the annals of history.

Epilogue

Six weeks later, Margaret's story, "The Sailing of the Ill-Fated Steamship Titanic," was published in the *Newport Herald* and *Denver Post*:

> *The last half-hour lapsing between the first and second gongs, when all take their exercise before descending to the dining hall, most of the passengers are to be found walking enveloped in heavy wraps. The women were in luxurious furs, and the men in heavy overcoats buttoned closely around their necks and partly disguised in steamer caps. In passing to and fro they discovered old friends on board, and some made new ones. Small groups were standing here and there, discussing the ship and its marvels, its possibility for speed, and all its wonderful advantages over anything of its kind heretofore put afloat…*
>
> *…After luncheon, or about two-thirty, the favorite and popular place was the reading room, where the passengers settled themselves comfortably with some chosen book from the well-equipped library on the ship. Others were taking a quiet siesta on the deck, wrapped in heavy steamer rugs. Few remained in their staterooms, for the sea was perfectly calm and no vibration was felt. Consequently, there was little or no mal-de-mer.*
>
> *Thus Thursday, Friday and Saturday were passed.*
>
> *Sunday services were held at ten-thirty, quite one-half of the passengers attending. Later the passengers went outside to promenade on deck, but much more briskly as the temperature had dropped perceptibly lower. After luncheon a few remained on deck, but all were restlessly searching for a warm place. The comfortable chairs in the lounge held but a few, as a shaft of cold air seemed to penetrate every nook and corner, and chill the marrow. Heavy furs and warm clothing were donned.*
>
> *Dinner time found few inclined to shed their warm clothing for dinner dress. Even the innumerable brides, who on various occasions appeared in a different Paris creation each night, could not be induced to change. Though the board groaned with viands, the passengers found it uncomfortable to sit through the many-course dinner. Many sought their staterooms immediately afterwards…*
>
> *…Anxious to finish a book I stretched on the brass bed at the side of which was a lamp. So completely absorbed in my reading, I gave little thought to the crash that struck at my window overhead and threw me to the floor. Picking myself up I proceeded to see what the steamer had struck. On emerging from the stateroom, I found many men in the gangway in their pajamas, whom I had overheard a few moments before entering their staterooms saying that they were nearly frozen and had to leave the*

smoking-rooms. They, while standing, were chaffing each other, one of them remarked, "Are you prepared to swim in those things?" referring to the pajamas. Women were standing along the corridors in their kimonos. All seemed to be quietly listening, thinking nothing serious had occurred, though realizing at the time that the engines had stopped immediately after the crash and the boat was at a standstill, and as there was no confusion of any kind, the book was again picked up.

On hearing the occupants of the adjoining stateroom say, "We will go on deck and see what has happened," I again arose and saw six or more stewards and one officer in the corridor forcing an auger through a hole in the floor, while treating the whole thing with levity. Again returning to my book, presently I saw the curtains moving, but no-one was visible.

I again looked out, and saw a man whose face was blanched, his eyes protruding, wearing the look of a haunted creature. He was gasping for breath, and in an undertone he gasped, "Get your life-saver." I immediately reached above my head and dragged all out, as I thought some others might need them. Snatching up furs, and placing a silk capote on my head, I hurriedly mounted the stairs to A deck, and there I found possibly fifty passengers, all putting on their life belts. Strapping myself into mine, I afterwards was told to go up on the storm deck.

My party that I was traveling with had already gone up. On reaching A deck, Mrs. Bucknell approached and whispered to me, "Didn't I tell you something was going to happen?" On reaching the storm deck we found a number of men trying to unravel the tackle of the boats to let them down, which seemed at the time very difficult. We were approached by an officer and told to descend to the deck below. We found the lifeboats there were being lowered from the falls and were at the time flush with the deck. Madame DeVallier, of Paris, appeared from below in a night dress and evening slippers with no stockings, over which she wore a woolen motor coat. She clutched at my arm and in a terrified voice said she was going below for her money and jewels. After much persuasion I prevailed upon her not to go down but to get into the boat. As she hesitated and became very excited, I told her it was all only a precaution and she would be able to return to the then-sinking steamer later. After she got on, I turned and found the lady of my party in a lowering boat. I was walking away eager to see what was being done with the boats on the other side, not fearing any immediate danger, thinking if the worst should happen I could swim out. Suddenly I saw a shadow, and a few seconds later I was taken hold of, and with the words, "You are going, too," I was dropped fully four feet into the lowering life-boat.

Epilogue

While being lowered by jerks by an officer from above, I discovered that a great gush of water was spouting through the porthole from D deck, and our lifeboat was in grave danger of being submerged. I immediately grasped an oar and held the lifeboat away from the ship. While being lowered we were conscious of strains of music being wafted on the night air. As we reached a sea as smooth as glass, we looked up and saw the benign, resigned countenance, the venerable white hair, and the Chesterfieldian bearing of our beloved Captain (with whom I had crossed twice before—only previous, on the Olympic, *our party sat at his table), as he peered down upon us like a solicitous father, directing us to row to the light in the distance, and all boats keep together. With but one man in the boat, and possibly fourteen women, I saw that it was necessary for someone to bend to the oars. I placed mine in the rowlocks, and asked a young woman near me to hold one while I placed the other one on the further side. To my surprise she immediately began to row like a galley-slave, every stroke counting. Myself on the other side we managed to pull out from the steamer. All the time while rowing we were facing the starboard side of the sinking vessel. By the time E and C decks were completely submerged, and the strains of music became fainter, as though the instruments were filling up with water. Suddenly all ceased when the heroic musicians could play no more.*

The only seaman in our boat was the quartermaster. He was at the rudder, and standing much higher than we were. He was shivering like an aspen. As we pulled away from the boat, we heard sounds of firing, and were told later that it was officers shooting as they were letting down the boats from the steamer, trying to prevent those from the lower decks jumping into the lifeboats. Others said it was the boilers…

…Presently we heard shouts and cries of terror from the fast sinking ship. We were told the shouts were from the trunk men on the collapsible boats. Our quartermaster haggled long and loud. The splash of the oars partly drowned the voices of the perishing men on the doomed steamer. The ladies all seemed terrified. Those having husbands, sons or fathers, buried their heads on the shoulders of those near them, and moaned and groaned only.

While my eyes were glued on the fast disappearing ship, I particularly watched the broad promenade deck. It was fully lighted but not one moving object was visible. Suddenly a rift in the water, the sea opened up and the surface foamed like giant arms spread around the ship, and the vessel disappeared from sight, and not a sound was heard.

Bibliography

Abandoned Rails. "The Hannibal and Saint Joseph Railroad." www.abandonedrails.com/Hannibal_and_Saint_Joseph_Railroad.

Ambler, Charles H. *Sectionalism in Virginia, 1778–1861*. Chicago: University of Chicago Press, 1910.

American Friends of Blerancourt. "History of the Museum." http://www.americanfriendsofblerancourt.org/history/index.html.

Bacon, Thomas H. *Mirror of Hannibal 1905*. Revised and reprinted by J. Hurley and Roberta (Roland) Hagood. Hannibal and Marceline, MO: Hannibal Free Public Library/Jostens, 1990.

Bancroft, Caroline. *The Unsinkable Mrs. Brown*. Boulder, CO: Johnson Publishing Company, 1963.

Banzhaf, Charles, and John L. Ransom. *History of Hannibal and City Directory, 1871–72*. Hannibal, MO: Winchell, Ebert and Marsh Printing Company, 1871.

Benziger, James George. "Memories of a Grandson." Unpublished manuscript, Molly Brown House Museum, Denver, Colorado.

Biel, Steven. *Down with the Old Canoe: A Cultural History of the Titanic Disaster*. New York: W.W. Norton & Company, 1996.

Blair, Edward. *Leadville: Colorado's Magic City*. Boulder, CO: Fred Pruitt Books, 1980.

Bloy, Marjorie. "A Web of English History: 'Less Eligibility.'" History Home. http://www.historyhome.co.uk/peel/poorlaw/eligibil.htm.

Bibliography

Boesen, Victor. *They Said It Couldn't Be Done: The Incredible Story of Bill Lear.* New York: Doubleday & Company, 1971.

Brown, Lawrence P. Scrapbook. Stephen H. Hart Library, Colorado Historical Society, Denver, Colorado.

Brown, Margaret T. "Shadows of Hindu Life." Published article, 1903. Found in Kristen Iversen's Brown biography.

Brown, Thomas J. *American Eras: Civil War and Reconstruction, 1850–1877.* New York: Manly, Inc., 1997.

Bucknell University. "History of Bucknell." http://www.bucknell.edu/x474.xml.

Burnett, Robyn, and Ken Luebbering. *German Settlement in Missouri: New Land, Old Ways.* Columbia: University of Missouri Press, 1996.

Butler, Daniel Allen. *Unsinkable: The Full Story of the RMS Titanic.* Mechanicsburg, PA: Stackpole Books, 1998.

Christensen, Lawrence O., William E. Foley, Gary E. Kremer and Kenneth H. Winn, eds. *Dictionary of Missouri Biography.* Columbia: University of Missouri Press, 1999.

Christman, Margaret C.S. *1846: Portrait of the Nation.* Washington, D.C.: Smithsonian Institution, 1996.

City of Galena. "History: City of Galena." www.cityofgalena.org/history.cfm.

Colton, G. Woolworth. *Map of the Hannibal & St. Joseph Railroad and Its Connections.* New York: American Railway Review, 1860.

Cork Guide. "Fermoy." http://www.cork-guide.ie/fermoy/index.htm.

Daily Missouri Republican. "Removing a City." November 16, 1841.

Davis, Kay. "Class and Leisure at America's First Resort." American Studies at the University of Virginia. http://xroads.virginia.edu/~ma01/davis/newport/newport%20history/newporthistory.html.

Dempsey, Terrell. *Searching for Jim: Slavery in Sam Clemens's World.* Columbia: University of Missouri Press, 2003.

Elliot, Maud Howe. *This Was My Newport.* Cambridge, MA: A. Marshal Jones, 1944.

Faherty, William Barnaby S.J. *The St. Louis Irish: An Unmatched Celtic Community.* St. Louis: Missouri Historical Society Press, 2001.

Fotheringham, H. *Hannibal City Directory for 1859–60.* Hannibal, MO: Wm. T. League & Company, 1859.

Fowler, Gene. *Timberline.* Garden City, NY: Garden City Publishing Company, 1933.

Garner, Edward. *To Die by Inches: The Famine in North East Cork.* Fermoy, County Cork, Ireland: Eigse Books, 1988.

Bibliography

Hagood, J. Hurley, and Roberta Hagood. *Hannibal's Yesterdays*. Marceline, MO: Jostens Publishing, 1992.

———. *Hannibal, Too: Historic Sketches of Hannibal and Its Neighbors*. Marceline, MO: Walsworth Publishing Company, 1986.

———. *The Story of Hannibal: A Bicentennial History, 1976*. Hannibal, MO: Hannibal Free Public Library/Standard Printing Company, 1976.

Hagood, J. Hurley, Roberta Hagood and Dave Thomson. *Hannibal Heritage*. Marceline, MO: Heritage House Publishing, 1994.

Hagood, J. Hurley, Roberta Hagood and Mary Lou Montgomery. *Hannibal Bridges the Mississippi*. Marceline, MO: Jostens Publishing, 2000.

Hannibal Historic Societies. "Friends of Historic Hannibal." Marion County, Missouri and Hannibal, Missouri Historic Groups. www.hannibalhistoricsocieties.org/FOHH.htm.

History of Recorded Technology. "Bill Lear Invents the 8-Track and Brings in Ford, Motorola, and RCA Victor." Recording History. www.recording-history.org/HTML/8track4.php.

Holcombe, R.I. *History of Marion County Missouri*. St. Louis, MO: E.F. Perkins, 1884.

Hyman, Tony. "Cigar Factories in 1885." National Cigar History Museum. http://cigarhistory.info/Cigarmaking/Cigar_factories_1885_I.html.

Isenberg, Nancy. "Women's Rights Movements." American National Biography Online and the Oxford Companion to United States History. http://www.anb.org/cush_rights.html.

Iversen, Kristen. *Molly Brown: Unraveling the Myth*. Boulder, CO: Johnson Printing, 1999.

Jensen, Oliver. *The American Heritage History of Railroads in America*. New York: American Heritage Publishing Company Inc., 1975.

Kilbane, Doris. "William Lear: Aviation Legend Makes Waves in Audio, Too." Electronic Design. http://electronicdesign.com/article/communications/william-lear-aviation-legend-makes-waves-in-audio-aspx.

Klistorner, Daniel. "Molly Brown: Mystery Unravelled." Encyclopedia Titanica. http://www.encyclopedia-titanica.org/molly_cabin.html.

Kluth, Andreas. "Hannibal, Fabius, and Scipio in Missouri." "The Hannibal Blog." http://andreaskluth.org/2010/05/13/hannibal-fabius-scipio-in-missouri.

Labode, Modupe. "A Carnival for a Cathedral: The 1906 Carnival of Nations in Denver." Academia.edu. http://www.academia.edu/483995/_A_Carnival_for_a_Cathedral_The_1906_Carnival_of_Nations_in_Denver.

Lake County Public Library, Leadville, CO. *Leadville City Directories, 1879–1888*. http://www.lakecountypubliclibrary.org/City%20Directories.htm.

Maltin, Tim, ed. *Titanic: First Accounts*. Afterword by Nicholas Wade. New York: Penguin Classics, 2012.

Mark Twain Boyhood Home & Museum. "Twain's Life and Works." www.marktwainmuseum.org/index.php/research/twains-life-and-works.

McClure, C.H. *History of Missouri*. Chicago: Laidlaw Brothers Inc., 1920.

McLachlan, Sean. *Missouri: An Illustrated History*. New York: Hippocrene Books Inc., 2008.

Miller, Julie, and Becky Olson. "Molly Brown" Genealogy Project. http://jpmres.fatcow.com/brown-browngenealogyproject.net.

Missouri Bureau of Labor Statistics. *Missouri, 1912–13–14: Resources, Advantages, and Opportunities of a Thriving Commonwealth*. Jefferson City, MO: Hugh Stevens Publishing Company, 1914.

Missouri State Archives and Charter Media. "Marie Byrum Video Transcript." *Moments in Missouri Political History Video Segments*. www.sos.mo.gov/mdh/mmh/transcripts/mmph_tsByrum.html?Submit=View+Transcript.

Modelski, Andrew W. *Railroad Maps of North America: The First Hundred Years*. Washington, D.C.: Library of Congress, 1984.

Motorola. "Music in Motion: The First Motorola-Branded Car Radio." www.motorola.com/Consumers/US-EN/About_Motorola/History/Explore_Motorola_Heritage/Music_In_Motion.

Musick, John Roy. *Stories of Missouri*. New York: American Book Company, 1897.

New York Times. "Papal Countess Annie Leary Dies." April 27, 1919. http://query.nytimes.com/mem/archive-free/pdf?res=F70815FA345F157A93C5AB178FD85F4D8185F9.

O'Grada, Cormac. "Ireland's Great Famine: An Overview." Centre for Economic Research, University College Dublin, November 2004. http://www.ucd.ie/economics/research/papers/2004/WP04.25.pdf.

O'Laughlin, Michael C. *Missouri Irish: The Original History of the Irish in Missouri*. Kansas City, MO: Irish Genealogical Foundation, 2007.

Oster, Donald B. "The Hannibal and St. Joseph Railroad, Government and Town Funding, 1846–1861." *Missouri Historical Review* 87, no. 4 (July 1993): 403–21.

O'Sullivan, Patrick. *The Irish World Wide*. Vols. 1–6. Leicester, England: Leicester University Press, 1992–97.

Overton, Richard C. *Burlington Route: A History of the Burlington Lines*. New York: Alfred A. Knopf, 1965.

Parrish, William E. *A History of Missouri: 1820–1860*. Columbia: University of Missouri Press, 2000.

———. *Turbulent Partnership: Missouri and the Union, 1861–1865*. Columbia: University of Missouri Press, 1963.

Powers, Ron. *Mark Twain: A Life*. New York: Free Press, 2005.

Prokopowicz, Gerald J. *American Eras: The Reform Era and Eastern U.S. Development, 1815–1850*. New York: Manly, Inc., 1998.

Ramsay, Robert Lee. *Our Storehouse of Missouri Place Names*. Columbia: University of Missouri Press, 1952.

Schlereth, Thomas J. *Victorian America: Transformations in Everyday Life, 1876–1915*. New York: HarperCollins Publishers, Inc., 1991.

Scott, Robert N., comp. *War of the Rebellion: A Compilation of the Official Records of the Union and Confederate Armies*. 128 vols. Washington, D.C.: Government Printing Office, 1900.

Stenhouse, Paul. "The Irish Penal Code." Sean Ó Lachtnáin's Home Page. http://jloughnan.tripod.com/irishpen.htm.

Stover, John F. *The Routledge Historical Atlas of the American Railroads*. New York: Routledge, 1999.

Twain, Mark. *Adventures of Huckleberry Finn: The Only Comprehensive Edition*. Foreword and Addendum by Victor Doyno. New York: Random House, 1996.

———. *The Adventures of Tom Sawyer*. New York: Oxford University Press, 1996.

Twain, Mark, and Charles Dudley Warner. *The Gilded Age*. New York: Quill Pen Classics, 2008.

United States Department of the Interior Heritage Conservation and Recreation Service. "National Register of Historic Places Inventory-Nomination Form: Central Park Historic District." Department of Natural Resources. www.dnr.mo.gov/shpo/nps-nr/80002377.pdf.

University of California [Berkeley] Museum of Paleontology. "Thomas Malthus." http://www.ucmp.berkeley.edu/history/malthus.html.

Walley, Dean. *Mark Twain by the Riverside—Favorite Sayings of Mark Twain*. Kansas City: April House Publishing, 1973.

Ward, Geoffrey C., and Ric Burns. *The Civil War: An Illustrated History*. New York: Alfred A. Knopf, Inc., 1990.

Weaver, H. Dwight. *Missouri Caves in History and Legend*. Columbia: University of Missouri Press, 2008.

Wikipedia. "Hannibal and St. Joseph Railroad." http://en.wikipedia.org/wiki/Hannibal_and_St._Joseph_Railroad.

———. "Steamboats of the Mississippi." http://en.wikipedia.org/wiki/Steamboats_of_the_Mississippi.

Williams, Walter, ed. *A History of Northeast Missouri.* 3 vols. Chicago: Lewis Publishing Company, 1913.

The Workhouse: Story of an Institution. "Fermoy, Co. Cork." http://www.workhouses.org.uk/Fermoy.

———. "The Workhouse in Ireland." http://www.workhouses.org.uk/Ireland.

Index

C

D

About the Authors

Ken and Lisa Marks were born and raised in St. Louis, Missouri, but are now full-fledged Hannibalians. They are the co-curators of the Hannibal History Museum in Hannibal's Main Street Historic District, where Lisa performs a historically accurate portrayal of Margaret Tobin Brown in the one-woman show *The Life and Times of Molly Brown*. Through their company, Historic Hannibal Tours, LLC, they offer guided historic tours and Haunted Hannibal Ghost Tours™.

The Markses are coauthors of two other books by The History Press: *Haunted Hannibal: History and Mystery in America's Hometown* (2010) and *Hannibal, Missouri: A Brief History* (2011). They are contributing writers for *Hannibal* magazine and *Missouri Life* magazine and are always available to lecture about all aspects of Hannibal's history.

Lifelong history fanatics, they are members of the Friends of Historic Hannibal, the Marion County Historical Society and the Historic Hannibal Marketing Council. They are lovingly restoring their Second Empire home (originally built for Judge Joseph Rowe) located on Sixth Street in the Central Park Historic District of Hannibal, just three blocks from Margaret Tobin Brown's birthplace on Denkler's Alley. They are committed to historic preservation and are working with other Hannibalians to preserve and protect the precious structures in Margaret Tobin Brown's hometown.